THE VIBRAPHONE AND THE BENDING TONE: A NEW APPROACH TO SOUND

by André Cayer © 2014

Graphic design (cover) : Julie Noël
Translation to English from French by Sebastien Obermeir

VIDEO & AUDIO ON

www.andrecayer.com

Oliphanz Productions – Sherbrooke, Qc. Canada

Toute reproduction, par quelque procédé que ce soit, est interdite.

Dépôt légal – 1er trimestre 2014 – Bibliothèque nationale du Québec
Bibliothèque nationale du Canada - ISBN 978-2-9814437-1-7

The translation of this document was made possible through the assistance of the Fonds d'appui à la création et l'édition d'une oeuvre savante of the Sherbrooke University.

Thanks to: Sherbrooke University, the faculty of literature and humanities and their music school for their support, to all people who participated to this project (Robert Leroux, Denis Gougeon, Julie et Sophie Cayer, Daniel Couture, Christiane Bolduc), and especially to Ann-Elisabeth for her great support.

Introduction 6

The vibraphone 7

History 7

Expecting results 7

1. Placing the hard mallets 8
1.1 Method according to type of grip used 8
1.2 Types of Mallets 10
1.3 Advantages and uses 10

2. Method for producing the bending tone on the vibraphone 12
2.1 The bending tone 12
2.2. Ideal range 12
2.3 Playing the bending tone in four steps 12
2.3.1 Playing the bending tone: placing the hard mallet 13
2.3.2 Producing the bending tone: Striking the bar 15
2.3.3 Playing the bending tone: sliding the mallet on the surface of the bar 16
2.3.4 Playing the bending tone: raising the mallet from the bar 21

3 Types of bending tone 22
3.1. Simple bending tone 22
3.2. Double bending tone 22
3.3 Repeated and off key note 23
3.4 Independent use of the hard mallet 23

4 Transitions and fingerings 24
4.1. Transition towards another note 24
4.2. The alternating bending tone 24
4.3 Parallel bending tones 24
4.4 Playing sliding passages 24
4.5 Fingerings 25
4.5.1 Basic fingerings on the same keyboard 25
4.5.2 Basic fingerings when changing keyboards 25
4.5.3 Basic fingerings for longer passages on the same keyboard 26
4.5.4 Basic fingerings for longer passages when changing keyboard 26
4.5.5 Basic fingerings for large intervals 27
4.5.6 Fingering chart 28

5. Other concepts 29
5.2. Using the pedal 29
5.3 Posture and fitness 29

6. Graphology and developing sound 31
6.1. Graphology 31
6.1.1. Hand used 31

○ = Strike with right hand (placement and sliding with left hand) 31
● = Strike with left hand (placement and sliding with right hand) 31
    6.1.2. Mallet numbers 31
    6.1.3. Simple bending tone 31
    6.1.4. Double bending tone 32
    6.1.5. Triple and quadruple bending tones 32
    6.1.6. Off-key bending tones 33
    6.1.7. Bending tone with strike from second hard mallet 33
    6.1.8. Bending tone striking the neutral point 33
    6..1.9. Bending tones with grace notes 33
6.2. Developing sound 34

Conclusion 36

Part two- Exercises 37
  1. Exercise introduction 37
  2. Exercise guide 37
  3. Steps for each exercise: 37
  4. Notes 37
  5. Exercises 38

Part three: Etudes 67
  ÉTUDE 1 68
  ÉTUDE 2 70
  ÉTUDE 3 72
  ÉTUDE 4 74
  ÉTUDE 5 76
  ÉTUDE 6 78
  ÉTUDE 7 80

THE VIBRAPHONE AND THE BENDING TONE: A NEW APPROACH TO SOUND
by André Cayer

Introduction

The vibraphone is one of the most versatile and fascinating instruments. It is for this reason that, despite its short history, it was able to create a very special place for itself in the musical world where jazz and classical music tend towards this increasingly elaborate unity. Indeed, in just a few short years, the vibraphone became a standard of modern music that introduced a repertoire that is increasingly adapted, as well as interesting and specialized composers and performers. Despite this, there is still much to be done before bestowing such gracious descriptions. In this context, this work, aiming the development of the musical palette, is meant as a contribution, I hope, which will open up whole new possibilities for the instrument.

This book explores the musical potential of one effect: the bending tone. It also includes concrete and efficient steps to playing the bending tone, and then leads to applying it smoothly and systematically in musical performances. This tools' potential shows a new way of looking at the instrument that is, in my opinion, much more expressive.

Here are some examples of advantages of using the bending tone:

- The possibility of playing a bending note with both hands while retaining all advantages of a mastered four-mallet grip.
- Greater flexibility which allows for:
    - Including bending tones in fast passages;
    - Including bending tones within four-note chords;
    - Striking one or two new notes in the same hand simultaneously while producing a bending tone just before;
    - Playing fast passages where each note slides;
    - Adding much more subtlety to a performance.
- An increased control of all steps to producing a bending tone;
- A smooth mix of all the different options between traditional and new sounds;
- Great potential leading to the development of new possibilities in musical technique such as:
    - Parallel (simultaneous) bending tones;
    - Controlled vibrato;
    - Off key notes
    - A bending tone followed by a four-note chord ;
    - Double and triple bending tones;
    - New sound alternatives sustained by the direct use of two extra mallets or heads.

The vibraphone

Due to the use of the pedal and the striking of notes, the vibraphone is often compared to the piano regarding technique and sound possibilities. It is, however, different from the latter because of its unique sound and its ability to choose which notes resonate thanks to dampening techniques and the motor.

Some say that the instrument offers rather limited musical possibilities. Indeed, the piano, with its' large range and polyphonic freedom, can make up for its lack of musical subtlety (compared to wind or string instruments). As for the vibraphone, it lacks (so some say) tools to widen its musical palette and this is the problem that an approach such as this one tries to address.

Indeed, with the use of this *method of note bending on the vibraphone*, possibilities for a richer sound seem to multiply and give life to each note all the while offering new developments in vibraphone technique.

History

Traditionally, the bending tone was used sporadically in some contemporary repertoires or in jazz. To do so, one would simply replace one of the mallets used while creating the desired effect. Because of the lack of flexibility of this approach (difficult switches between mallets, limited by having one less mallet, difficulty of execution, etc.), the bending tone has been used sparingly until now.

Expecting results

Firstly, this approach incorporates a new element in the traditional mallet grip. Indeed, a hard mallet head (or a short xylophone mallet) will add itself to the end of another mallet. This addition can be made with any style of grip (see section on *mallet grips*).

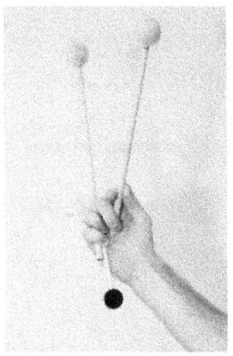

This addition has already been made somewhat sporadically by certain musicians, but its development within traditional and virtuoso technique now appears to me as indispensible since the possibilities of this "third mallet" greatly surpasses a simple purpose that consisted traditionally in striking an instrument other than the vibraphone (such as crotales or a triangle, etc.).

In fact, the originality of this approach resides essentially in the unique fashion in which this "third mallet" is used, since it allows the effect of the bending tone to be formalized and developed, requiring both a hard mallet and a regular vibraphone mallet.

This method therefore has two goals: First of all, to introduces the use of six mallets[1] as a perfectly sustainable and adaptable solution to different styles, and then to present an easy approach to the bending tone which ultimately allows the development of new musical potential.

This volume also dedicates a chapter to composers interested in new acoustic possibilities linked to the development of the bending tone on the vibraphone. You will find there information concerning graphology as well as sound exploration associated to the techniques elaborated upon.

The second part of this method offers a series of exercises related to the different techniques found in the first part. Each one is accompanied, if necessary, with advice on how to properly play them. However, reading the first part of the method is necessary to proper understanding and adequate performance of the exercises.

Finally, the third part consists of a collection of etudes associated with the different techniques seen in this method.

Part 1 – Creating the bending tone

1. Placing the hard mallets

We will not compare types of grips that are a personal choice since **this method applies to all types**, no matter which one is chosen (two mallets, Musser, Burton, extended cross grip, traditional, etc.) or the method of movement chosen (Stevens, Burton, fulcrum, Morel, etc.). Indeed, the techniques developed here do not affect freedom of movement or virtuosity.

> *"As for me, I chose the Musser grip (based on the method of movement developed by Leigh Howard Stevens). In order to add volume and flexibility in the way I play, I chose to shorten my mallets, which results in what seems to me as increased musical possibilities. Obviously, while this method works very well on the vibraphone, it may be otherwise for the marimba that requires, due to its size, a considerably longer mallet."*
> A. Cayer

1.1 Method according to type of grip used

According to certain conditions, a shorter mallet with a hard head (of the xylophone type) is simply added to the opposite end of one of the mallets already in place[2].

Here is how it can be done according to the grip used

1.1.1 Simple grip (2 mallets)

Choose between a double sided mallet with one hard headed end or adding a shorter hard headed mallet to the end of both your mallets. You may opt to place the new mallet, if the case may be, inside the palm so as to avoid movement of the hard mallet due to its weight. The ideal length of the new mallet should be about 19 cm (7.5"), allowing a balanced weight distribution and a less cumbersome grip (see figure below).

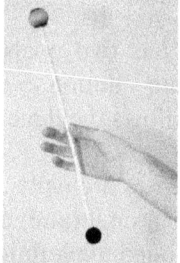 

1.1.2 Burton style grip

Those who use the Burton style grip simply add a hard head to each of the two exterior mallets. This way, the shaft with the extra hard head will be in direct contact with the palm, which allows an increased weight without effort (while playing, the shaft of the hard mallet should follow the arms movements).

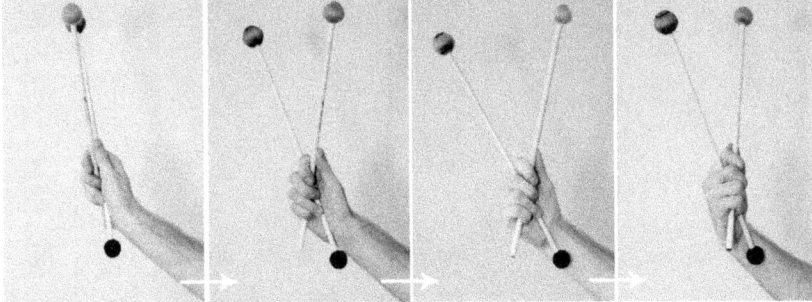

1.1.3 Musser style grip (Stevens technique)

In the case of the Musser style grip, the two extra mallets or hard heads (according to preference) will be placed at the inverted extremities of each exterior mallet (1 and 4) as explained lower.

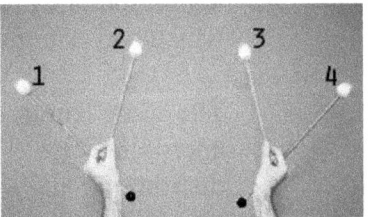

In fact, there are two possible choices for the Musser style user:

a) Use the longer mallets on the exterior (1 and 4) of which one extremity contains the hard head and the other, the normal head.

While efficient, this approach is difficult to consider for those who use long shafts because it requires the use of custom made mallets (approximately 8cm or 3" more than the length of the interior mallets).

The shaft along the 4th metacarpal (bone) and the resting point is found against the pisiform bone. As is the case for the Burton grip, the shaft with the hard head will therefore be in direct contact with the base of the hand, which increases the weight with very little effort.

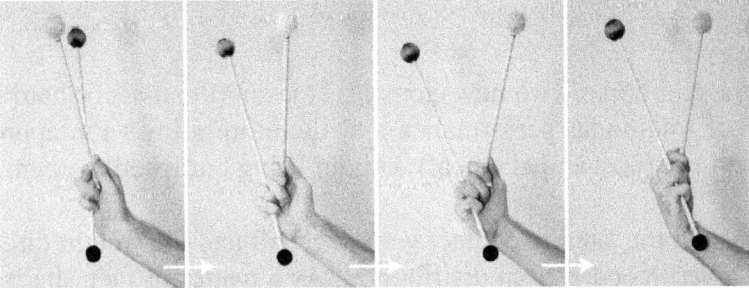

a) The second possibility appears to me as the most versatile since it offers multiple combinations. It functions by adding two new, very short mallets and to place them inverted with the exterior mallets (1 and 4). For an optimal grip, you may choose to insert the shaft on the inside (in direct contact with the skin) so as to avoid displacement of the mallet, which would make performance difficult.

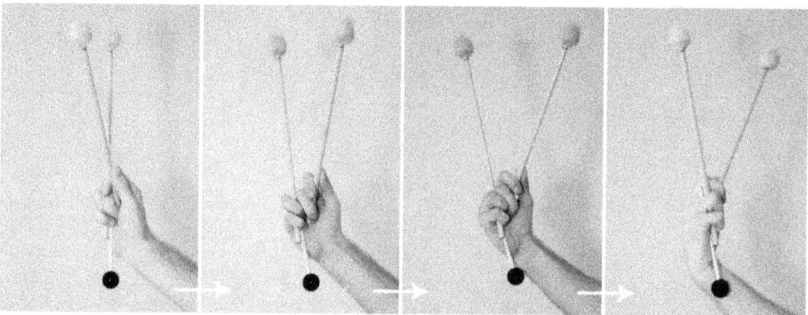

Again, the two long shafts follow the 4th metacarpal (bone) and the resting point of the hard mallet is found against the pisiform bone, which adds weight with almost no effort.

The ideal length of the new mallet should be, including the head, approximately 17cm (6.5"), allowing both a good weight distribution and a less cumbersome grip. Rattan appears to me as a very efficient solution for the new shaft since it allows a natural adjustment of the point of contact of the hard head and the bar as well as weight distribution.

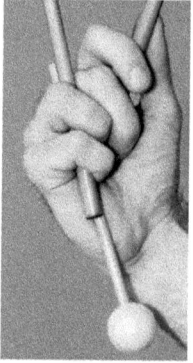

Finally, the shaft should be thin enough to have a good grip of both mallets simultaneously by the outside fingers. After a few hours of practice, you will forget about them altogether.

1.2 Types of Mallets

Concerning the type of head used, avoid using a soft material that stops the vibration of the bar (black rubber, for example). Likewise, a head that is too hard will disconnect the vibrating bar, creating an undesirable noise. Personally, certain types of plastic heads seem to me like the most efficient so far. This is a matter of taste.

1.3 Advantages and uses

As previously explained, the addition of two new elements (the short mallets or hard heads) does not change the flexibility of traditional performance and therefore allows the approach of the entirety of the existing repertoire (jazz and classical) without being burdened by them.

Furthermore, having the base of the hand in contact with the shaft and the weight directly created by the forearm allows for a very good weight distribution. As a matter of fact, the final result is greatly improved since there is more control.

Using such a grip on other percussion keyboards is, in my opinion, equally possible and even desirable since, for the reasons mentioned above, it allows to extend the possibilities of the instrument. For example:

- Pieces using exterior elements (crotales, triangles, anvils, etc.) requiring the use of hard mallets;
- Pieces with simple passages to be played on other keyboard instruments (xylophone, glockenspiel, etc.);
- Setups requiring the performer to cover different types of surfaces;
- Varied combinations of mallet types (4+2; 2+2+2; 4+1+1; etc.)

2. Method for producing the bending tone on the vibraphone

2.1 The bending tone
The bending tone technique allows the gradual descent of the fundamental note of a vibrating bar by slowing its vibration. In order to create this effect, a hard mallet must be placed on the neutral point (above the rope), then slid along it after a second mallet has struck the bar. The simultaneous vibration of the hard head and of the bar ultimately produces a bending of sound capable of reaching one semi-tone lower.

During every step to create the bending tone, the pedal must be pressed, since the bending tone needs the vibration of that note.

Also, in all but exceptions, the body's position must not change with the integration the following techniques. It is a matter of simply incorporating the new techniques to those already being used without altering the original method of movement.

Finally, as we will see in detail, many factors such as the striking point, the type of bending tone or the chosen range will influence the result of the sound.

2.2. Ideal range
The bending tone is possible anywhere on the vibraphone but may be more difficult in more extreme ranges. This is why the exercises in the second part concentrate on the central part of the instrument in order to facilitate learning. After, you may widen and even discover new musical possibilities linked to the choice of different ranges.

2.3 Playing the bending tone in four steps
Note: the contents of this method are usable on all types of vibraphones. However, results may vary depending on the type and brand of vibraphone used. Indeed, some instruments will create more or less harmonics, others won't resonate as long, etc. It will be (as it always is!) up to the instrumentalist to adapt him or herself to these minor differences.

2.3.1 Playing the bending tone: placing the hard mallet

2.3.1.1 Placing the hard mallet in the right place (two possibilities)
The first step consists of placing the hard mallet on the bar in such a way that it may continue vibrating. To do so, there are two strategic points where the vibration is almost inexistent and that corresponds to the path of the rope towards the bar (on both ends of the bar). These two areas are known as the nodal points (knots of the vibrating surface).

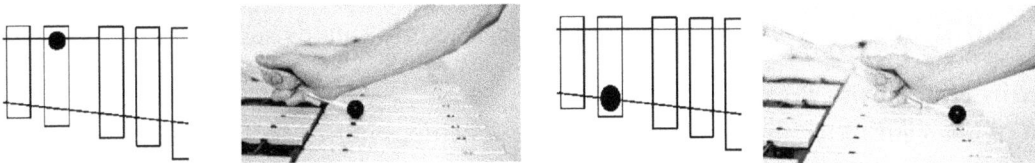

Once these surfaces are found, it is a matter of pressing the hard mallet onto it, without touching the instrument in any other way.

2.3.1.2 Silence
Unless a specific effect is desired, an ideal placement will be done on a bar that is not vibrating (and is therefore silent) in order to avoid undesired noises. The greatest challenge consists of placing the hard head silently.

Note: Even if it may sometimes seem easier to place the mallet after having leaned it on the side of the hand, this can eventually become a crutch since it makes the movement much slower. It is therefore preferable to have the habit from the start of placing the mallet directly on the bar without preparation.

2.3.1.3 Strategic angle and position of the mallet
Firstly, it is important to find the most strategic point to place the mallet.
At that time, a few questions arise:

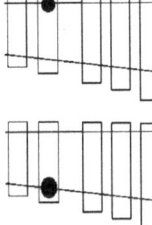

- In which direction will my bending tone go? In other words, what note am I aiming for?
- Which area will allow for the most efficient movement (distance, ease of movement, fluidity, etc.)?
- What kind of bending tone do I want to create?
- Will I have enough space to strike the bar with another mallet?

After a while, the answers to these questions will be practically automatic and the choice will be second nature.

As to the angle of the mallet to use for optimal results, the simplest way consists of placing the head in a way that the mallet is almost parallel with the keyboard. This way, the mallet will already be in place for the next three steps.

Note: It may happen that, following the placement, you must free space in the middle of the bar with a slight rotation of a few centimeters in the opposite direction of the mallet that will strike the note. In this case, immediately after striking, retract the hand in a way that the mallet is in the same direction as the bar. This movement of the hand will be used mostly when the placement is made on the rope of the bottom of the bar closest to the musician. This results in a small rotation with almost no effect on the vibration.

With practice, the hand will position itself naturally from the start in order to leave space for the mallet to strike, i.e. with a slight angle. Before proceeding to the second step, you must verify if space was cleared in order to avoid all risks of injury or eccentric sounds such as "ouch!"

2.3.1.4 The direction of the shaft
The direction of the shaft of the mallet (up or down) will be determined by the actions before and after it. In general, the simplest position will be the body's natural position, which is placing the hard head between the musician and the shaft and that, even on the upper keyboard.

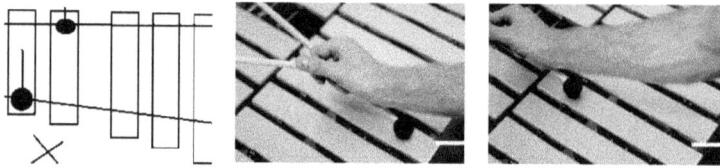

In some cases, the mallet must be placed in the opposite direction in order to allow a more fluid movement from the upper keyboard and on the furthest rope from the musician, which allows, for example, to strike the first keyboard with the other mallets of the same hand (inverted position).

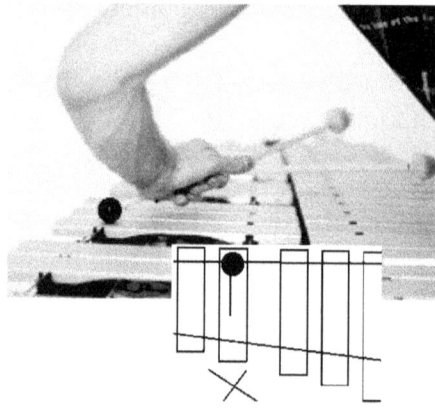

2.3.1.5 Placement in two steps
The placement step has two actions:

   a) The **contact with the surface** gently in the right place in order to avoid making noise. This action must be done as subtly as possible and requires control in the movement right before contact.
   b) As soon as the head touches the bar, **apply additional pressure** (weight) to avoid undesirable sounds that could be caused when striking the bar with the other mallet.

To increase the mastery of this crucial step, I suggest simply practicing its execution on the surfaces of bars or using any simple etudes you come across (for example *Délécluse* for the xylophone[3]) and to play all notes in complete silence by placing the heads in the rights places and practicing the two actions previously explained (**1- gently placing 2- pressure**). For the more determined, using any metallic surface is also possible (pots turned upside down, etc.).

If, in the beginning, it seems arduous, this step quickly becomes second nature for those who practice regularly.

2.3.1.6 Required pressure

Significant pressure is particularly important when striking the bar with another mallet because it is at that moment that the vibration is the most intense. Once applied, you may release some of the pressure in order to allow the note to resonate a bit longer if desired.

An optimal pressure will depend on the goals of the musician. If too intense, the result will be stifling the sound. If too light, undesired noises may be heard from the mallet head bouncing on the vibrating note.

The vibraphoniste may control the results according to his desires by adjusting the parameters, for example:

- Stifle the note before going to the next or;
- Pausing at the rope before making a bending tone (in this case, releasing the pressure right after striking the note, then applying it again before continuing with the bending tone);

2.3.2 Producing the bending tone: Striking the bar

As soon as the hard mallet is placed correctly with enough pressure and the target is clear, you may begin the second step: Striking.

This is the simplest of the four parts since it is simply striking the surface with another mallet while maintaining pressure with the first.

2.3.2.1 Where to strike

Depending on the circumstances and the desired sound, there are several possible areas to strike.

- **The centre of the bar** offers the most vibration as well as the richest sound. For these reasons, striking this area is offers the most possibilities (quality, duration, etc.) for the bending tone to come;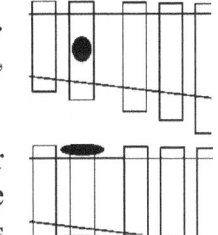

- **The ends of the bar** can be excellent alternatives when the centre is, for certain reasons (flexibility, speed, etc.), more difficult to reach. In this case the bending tone will be almost as successful. It is important, however, to strike as far away as possible from the rope in order to maximize the quality of the sound.

- Striking **along the rope** offers a much more muffled sound all the while emphasizing the type of strike on the note. The same techniques apply when creating the bending tone but the result will be more subtle. The rope offers less vibration and therefore less possibilities;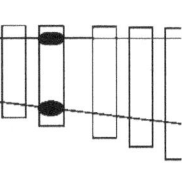

- Finally, it is also possible to choose to strike somewhere between the areas noted above. This allows for a compromise between qualities already mentioned.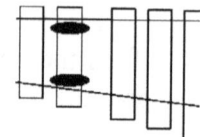

2.3.2.2 Choice of mallets or other objects to strike with

The choice of mallets is infinite and depends on a multitude of criteria ranging from personal taste to particular circumstances. It is also possible to strike the note with other objects like the other hard head, the shaft or even fingers. These techniques offer other very interesting options for sound.

It must be reminded, however, that the possibilities of the bending tone (length and quality of sound) are directly associated with the quality of the vibration in the bar. So, for example, an excessively soft mallet will produce a very muffled sound but offers much less freedom in creating the bending tone. It is therefore a question of esthetic choice.

2.3.2.3 Possible issues while striking

For the Musser type grip users (Stevens method) that use two extra mallets, you may sometimes hear sounds from the two shafts held with the little finger and ring finger hitting each other. In order to solve this problem, the little finger must be in contact with the shaft of the extra mallet while applying more pressure on it. This small detail will keep the two shafts together and prevent undesirable noises;
- Missing the note (for example: hitting your hand or another note): It happens! Increase the space between the note and the hand making the bending tone;
- The sound muffles itself instantly: Revue the placement of the hard mallet in order to maximize the vibration of the bar;
- Clicking sound coming from the bar: The placement was incorrect or there was not enough pressure on the hard mallet, which causes it to bounce on the bar.
-

2.3.3 Playing the bending tone: sliding the mallet on the surface of the bar

Sliding the mallet can be done from the moment the bar is struck. Then, simply move the hard mallet on the surface while maintaining a constant pressure with the wrist on the mallet, creating a change in the vibration of the bar. This movement should be as natural as possible.

2.3.3.1 Delaying the movement (neutral point)

There are two choices once the bar is struck: either **1- slide immediately** or **2- wait before sliding.**

The idea of delaying will be useful when, for example, you want to strike another note before sliding. It may also be interesting to use it to add expressiveness to the chosen note in order to first have a "free" note followed by a lyrical effect.

This delay can last for as long as the bar is vibrating (up to several seconds). Keep in mind that the following slide must also be sustained by the same vibration. It is for that reason important to evaluate what the desired result will be after this delay in order to have enough vibration to produce it.

Succeeding after this delay is therefore a direct result of the quality of the vibration linked to:

- The quality of the placement;
- The area chosen to strike;
- The pressure applied on the bar with the hard mallet.

2.3.3.2 Possible movements along the bar

- The simplest displacement (basic movement) is done starting from the rope and towards the centre of the bar and creates a bending tone of about a ½ tone;
- The same result may be obtained by starting from the upper rope and towards the centre.
- Starting from the rope and going towards the ends of the rope will also create a ½ tone bend but offers less possibilities and musical subtleties given that it makes the vibration stop much faster.
- The arrival point may differ since it is obviously possible to continue or stop sliding at anytime along the bar[4].

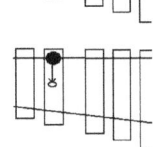
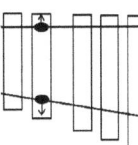

2.3.3.3 The direction of the shaft

From the basic position chosen during placement, it is possible to move the mallet according to three types of displacement: Parallel displacement, displacement at an angle and rotating displacement

2.3.3.3.1 Parallel displacement

Parallel displacement is done according to three basic movements that follow the direction given during placement[5].

a) First movement

For example, if the mallet is placed in a way that the head is between the musician and the shaft, follow the direction of the bar.

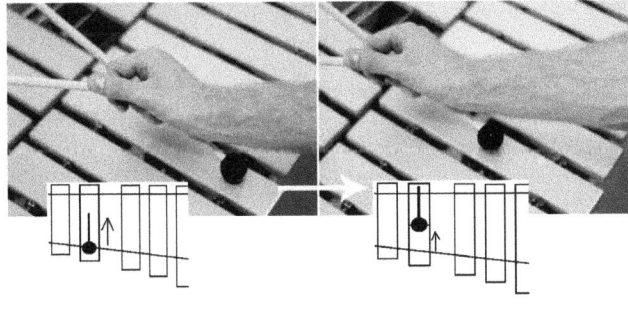

b) Second movement

The next situation presents itself when the placement is made on the furthest rope from the musician. The movement is in a parallel motion as well. However, unlike the first option (a forward movement), this time the weight of the wrist pushes the mallet towards the centre of the bar (towards the musician). Even if this may seem difficult in the beginning, this movement is worth practicing and mastering since it allows you to eventually develop flexibility similar to the first movement.

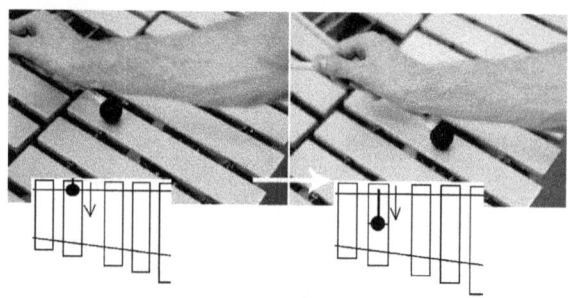

c) Third movement

Finally, you may be forced to reverse the direction of the mallet (shaft between the musician and the hard head). In this case, the bending tone will be played by following the given direction during placement as seen below. This will allow you to reach the lower notes of the keyboard with more fluidity.

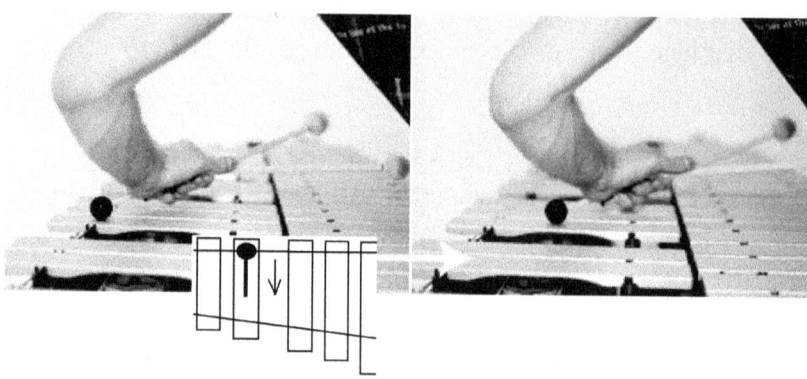

2.3.3.3.2 Displacement at an angle

The second type of movement simply copies the three movements developed in the parallel displacement but has an angle between the bar and the mallet. This will allow, for example, to prepare the strike of the next note with the hand creating the bending tone or to free the surface[6].

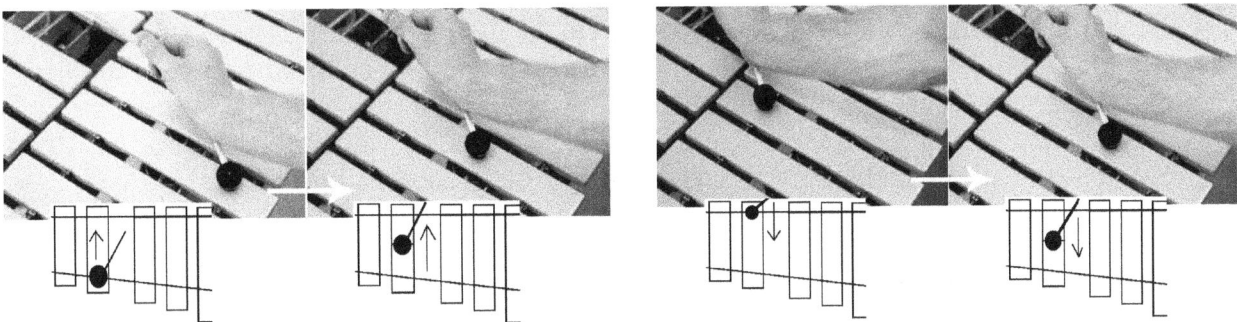

2.3.3.3.3 Rotating displacement

Finally, the third type of displacement repeats the first three basic movements while requiring a simultaneous rotation. This allows to anticipate, when necessary, the next note struck by the hand performing the sliding motion.

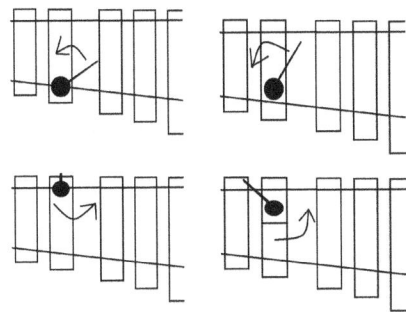

Unlike the two first types of displacements, this one requires you to change the angle of the mallet during its execution.

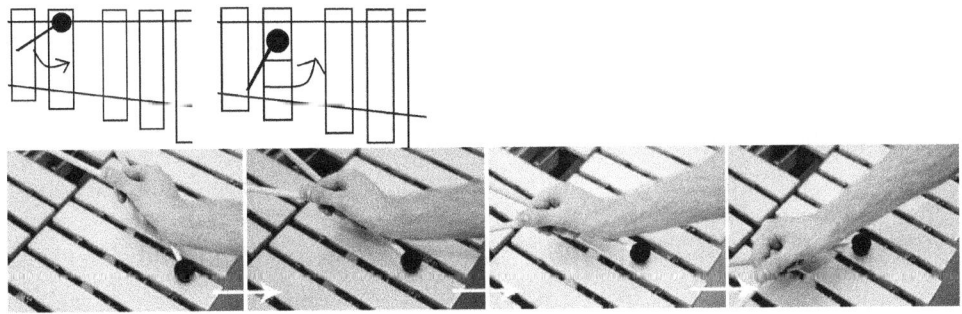

2.3.3.4 Area of displacement and arrival of the bending tone
The area of displacement and the point of arrival depend on the type of bending tone chosen.

2.3.3.5 Speed of performance
The speed of performance will also vary according to the desired result. It is however important to remember that from the moment that the sliding motion is performed (head starting at the knot (rope)), the vibration of the bar immediately starts to diminish, which leaves very little time for very slow effects. The delaying technique developed previously[7] will help increase or vary the impression of slowness sometimes required in certain circumstances or musical passage.

2.3.3.6 Required pressure
The required pressure when sliding varies according to certain circumstances (esthetic choice, range, type of mallet, etc.). You can generally adjust the strength by imagining the mallet cutting into the note, somewhat like soft butter. Indeed, visualizing it can be very useful in order to associate correctly the desired musical result with a tactile or mental image.

Specific information concerning the range of the instrument:

- The middle range of the vibraphone offers the best possibilities for the bending tone and finding the correct pressure is easy;
- For extreme ranges, it is sometimes necessary to make an adjustment in order to have a similar result. Because of the different vibration (slower in the low range and faster in the high range), the volume of the bending tone is slightly diminished and the harmonics tend to stand out more, which, without proper control, might make undesirable sounds. The pressure will therefore need to be adjusted (usually increased) and will require special care.
- It is also possible to vary the pressure in order to obtain different sound qualities. For example, in the lower range of the instrument, by releasing the weight on the mallet it is possible to bring out high-pitched harmonics, which offers an entirely different sound.

In summary, it is important to adapt the pressure exerted according to the range and even according to the vibraphone used. Certain types of bending tones will be much more difficult to produce in the extremes but are generally accessible throughout the instrument.

2.3.3.7 Possible problems while sliding
- Undesirable sounds due to the hard head and the bar hitting each other is usually because the wrong amount of pressure was applied. In this case, there is no special solution other than practicing and being one with the instrument. With time, you will be able to feel the pressure required to obtain the desired results (esoteric but realistic!);
- Sometimes, the cleanliness of the surface of the bar may be the source of similar problems. In this case, all it takes is cleaning;

- Finally, the material of the hard head may also influence the quality of the bending tone. For example, the rubber will have a tendency to stick to the bar and therefore stop the vibration.

2.3.4 Playing the bending tone: raising the mallet from the bar

You may have realized that at each step, the final goal is to control, as much as possible, the bars' vibration. This fourth step is no exception and is very important since it is the transition to the next note.

In general, there are two ways of finishing a bending tone and leaving the vibrating surface: stopping the pressure with increased pressure or letting the bar resume vibrating freely.

The first option is the most simple since it avoids any undesirable noises that can be caused by the separation of the mallet and the vibrating bar. In addition, stopping the vibration with a hard head reduces the use of conventional choking techniques.

This option requires a good feeling of the vibration of the bar in order to increase the necessary pressure to reduce the vibration at the right time. For example, you may increase the weight when approaching the end of the bending tone in a way that the end of it coincides with the end of the sound as well as the striking of the next note.

It is also possible to allow the bar to vibrate freely at the end of the bending tone. This technique is more complex because it requires leaving the vibrating surface without making undesirable noises from the hard head and the bar hitting each other. To do so, you must simply try to react as fast as possible.

Note that this technique is helped by returning to the rope (knot) or by a weaker vibration that allows a gentler release (see next chapter).

Finally, you can also literally "leave" the note by sliding towards the end of the bar until the mallet is no longer touching it.

3 Types of bending tone

3.1. Simple bending tone

The simple bending tone is characterized by the ½ tone descent. Its arrival point when sliding is at the **centre** or the **end** of the bar.
It may be used in two ways:

- To simply fill the gap between two notes since this type of bending tone may be used between any ascending or descending interval. The most efficient bending tones are the ones played at a descending interval, however. Optimally, the ½ tone interval is privileged;
- The simple bending tone is also efficient when used continuously, either during passages or series of intervals. Used in faster speeds, you may momentarily hear sounds similar to effects from the motor, which allows for more independence of the two voices by creating a very different sound quality between the two musical lines.

3.2. Double bending tone

The double bending tone essentially copies the techniques of the simple one but, instead of stopping at the centre of the bar, it continues to the opposite rope. This bending tone contains two parts: Lowering by a ½ tone (between the rope and the centre) followed by going back up a half tone (between the centre and the other rope) which returns to the original note.
A similar result may be obtained in two other ways:

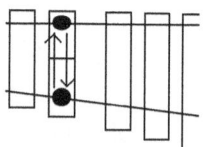

- By "leaving" the note, i.e. by sliding from the rope towards the end of the bar and continuing until the mallet is no longer touching its surface (returning to the original note more subtly).
- By going back and forth between the rope and the centre or the end of the bar (less vibration heard).

It is also possible to control, approximately, the rhythm of the three notes that stand out from the others in this type of bending tone (the original note, the note ½ tone beneath it and the return to the original note). It is a simple matter of changing the speed while playing very simple rhythmic figures[8].

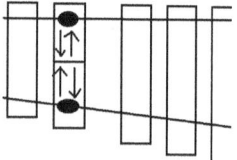

The double bending tone may be used in several ways:

- It can be used simply as an effect since the pitch of the sound returns to its starting point at the end and does not necessarily give an impression of direction or movement;
- It can also be used to slide from one note towards a higher note. Indeed, this embellishment towards the bottom can give the momentum to reach a higher pitch;
- Done continuously (continuous back and forth between the two ropes), this bending tone will create the same effect as when using the motor.

Just like the simple bending tone, it is also efficient when used repeatedly, either throughout passages or series of intervals.

Finally, this bending tone can be lengthened into a triple bending tone by simply continuing the sliding motion towards the end of the bar. The result is a series of roughly four sounds: the normal note, the note ½ tone lower, the return to the normal note and then again to the note ½ tone lower. In this case, the effect of the double-flourish ending at the bottom can offer momentum towards a lower pitch. You can even continue the movement by "leaving" the vibrating surface, which will result in a return to the original note (quadruple bending tone)[9].

3.3 Repeated and off key note

The repeated and off key note is in fact the result of sliding while striking the note repeatedly. The result is the impression of several descending note progressively leaving the original tone. This type of bending tone can be used to create different effects and has interesting advantages since striking repeatedly keeps the vibration in the bar and the rhythmic possibilities are infinite.

Repeated and off key bending tones can be used in several ways because:

- The number of strikes during the bending tone may vary, allowing, for example, to add different effects to a series of notes.
- The repeated note is good at emphasizing a delay (by slowing the strikes) or to accelerate (opposite).

3.4 Independent use of the hard mallet

The direct use of the hard mallet offers a multitude of unique and very interesting musical possibilities, while also allowing the use of other instruments in a setup (crotales, triangle, cymbal, glockenspiel, xylophone, anvil, etc.).

Furthermore, it is possible to create what I call the direct bending tone, meaning that the hard mallet strike comes from a loud placement by the rope while immediately applying pressure and sliding. This series of movements is done with a single hand. The resonance won't last as long but the musical result is worth it.

Finally, sound exploration linked to the independent use of the hard mallet is almost endless:

- It can be used to strike the surface of the bar directly (very clear and percussive sound);
- It is also possible to play bending tones while striking with the other hard mallet;
- Striking the bar with the hard mallet directly can also be joined with a strike from a soft mallet to be used as a flourish;
- You can also emphasize harmonics of the note by lightly pressing a mallet in the middle of the bar and striking one of the two ropes;

To finish, all sorts of possible combinations and uses with the hard mallet can be explored since they add to the richness of the musical language.

4 Transitions and fingerings

4.1. Transition towards another note

There are two different techniques to strike the note following a bending tone:

   a) **With the hand that made the sliding motion** (the same hand is simultaneously used to slide (with the hard mallet) and to strike (with one of the two normal mallets));
   b) **With the hand that already struck**, where repeating the action is required (same function with each hand).

The first option will result in an alternating bending tone, while the second will, among other things, be used to play melodic lines.

4.2. The alternating bending tone

Using the mallet grip explained earlier (chapter 1), the next note can be struck with the same hand playing the glissando along the bar. While the first hand is sliding, the second can place its mallet and prepare itself for the strike from the first hand. Repeated several times, these movements create an alternating bending tone.

It is sometimes much easier to strike the end of a bar instead of attempting complex movements to reach the center, especially when trying to reach the upper part of the keyboard from the bottom. Hence, mastering all types of displacements is very useful.

4.3 Parallel bending tones

Parallel bending tones (two simultaneous bending tones) are possible with the mastery of delaying before the movement (neutral point). It is a matter of:

   a) Placing the first hard mallet along the rope of a bar and striking it with another mallet. Do not slide yet;
   b) Placing the second hard mallet on another bar (the first still waiting);
   c) Striking the second bar with one of the free mallets of the first hand;
   d) Sliding along both notes simultaneously.

4.4 Playing sliding passages

The bending tone can also be used recurrently during melodic lines, imitating the use of the motor[10]. This technique is used, for example, to separate musical lines to add a particular sound to a portion of the melody. To do so, it is possible to use special fingerings that allow to slide on several nearby notes with one hand and that offer more flexibility in playing longer passages (scales, modes, series, arpeggios, etc.). The goal of these fingerings is to minimize useless movements capable of hindering playing sequences of bending tones.

4.5 Fingerings

4.5.1 Basic fingerings on the same keyboard

As previously explained, the placement is possible from two starting points: the upper or lower rope. With this in mind, there are four choices of fingerings that the performer can choose from to chain bending tones on two adjoining pitches (on the same keyboard) and with the same hand:

Note: the black dots signify the placement while the arrows show the sliding displacements (dark arrows) and the displacements in the air (pale arrows). Striking with another mallet is implied in the figure[11].

a) From bottom to top (first note) and from top to bottom (second note):

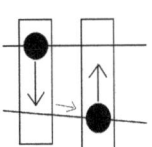

b) From top to bottom (first note) and from bottom to top (second note):

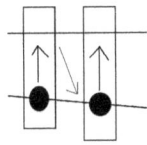

The next two fingerings can be used to fix or to interchange within a sequence of bending tone and prepare the approach of a note that is, for example, on the other keyboard:

c) Form bottom to top (first note) and from bottom to top (second note):

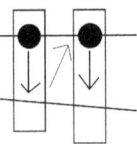

d) From top to bottom (first note) and from top to bottom (second note):

4.5.2 Basic fingerings when changing keyboards

Consecutive bending tones with the same hand when moving from one keyboard to the other, by a tone or ½ tone, are for their part usually played with two main fingerings:

From the lower keyboard to the upper one:

a) From bottom to top (first note) and from bottom to top (second note):

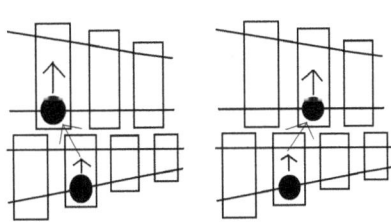

From the upper keyboard to the lower one:

    b) From top to bottom (first note) and from top to bottom (second note):

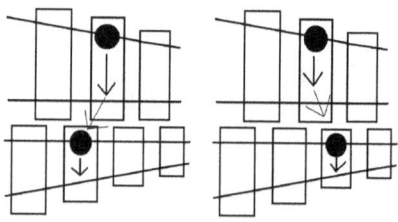

Note: There are other possible but much less efficient fingerings. Indeed, these fingerings encourage an efficiency of movement while avoiding useless changes in direction.

4.5.3 Basic fingerings for longer passages on the same keyboard
Playing the segment below uses the *basic fingerings on the same keyboard* previously illustrated. Each hand keeps its function (striking or sliding).

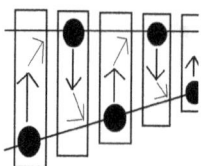

4.5.4 Basic fingerings for longer passages when changing keyboard
Combining the *basic fingerings on one keyboard* and the *basic fingerings when changing keyboards* makes playing longer passages (three or more sounds) possible. Here are the four basic fingerings which makes playing scales, modes, series and arpeggios now possible. Each hand will also retain its function (striking or sliding).

Towards the upper keyboard going up:

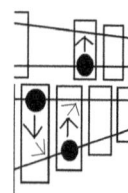

Towards the upper keyboard going down:

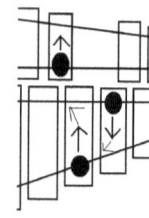

Towards the lower keyboard going up:

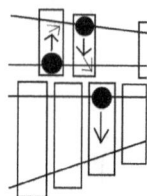

Towards the lower keyboard going down:

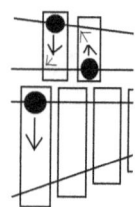

4.5.5 Basic fingerings for large intervals

Finally, controlling large intervals will also be very useful in some cases. It is a simple matter of using the *basic fingerings on one keyboard* and increasing the interval (3rd, 4th and up):

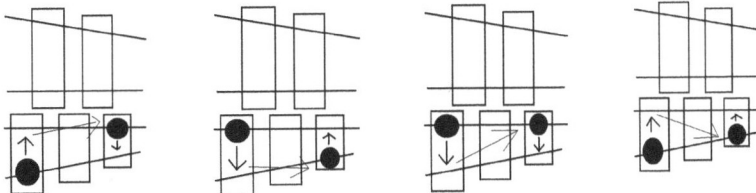

Large intervals with the same hand are also possible between two keyboards:

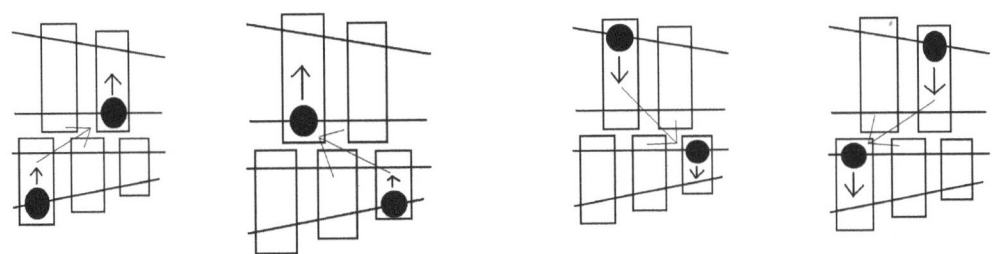

4.5.6 Fingering chart
Generally, the simplest approach consists of using one hand for each keyboard in order to avoid them crossing which would impact fluidity of movement. However, the *fingerings for longer passages when changing keyboards* may be very useful, especially when there are many large intervals (such as in certain modes).

○ = Right hand strike (placement and sliding with the left hand)
● = Left hand strike (placement and sliding with the right hand)
Here is a fingering chart with a few scales and major and minor arpeggios:

Note: The two choices differ according to the starting hand and correspond to the passage going from bottom to top. The first column offers the simplest possibility and the second is a more complex but more efficient alternative for faster passages.

Major Keys :
C :	○○○○○○○○	and	●●●●●●●●			
C# and D :	○○●○○○●○	and	●●○●●●○●	○○●●●●○○	and	●●○○○○●●
Eb and E :	○●●○○●●○	and	●○○●●○○●	○●●●●○○○	and	●○○○○●●●
F :	○○○●○○○○	and	●●●○●●●●	○○○○●●●●	and	●●●●○○○○
F# :	○○○●○○●○	and	●●●○●●○●			
G :	○○○○○○●○	and	●●●●●●○●			
Ab and A :	○○●○○●●○	and	●●○●●○○●	○○●●●○○●	and	●●○○○●●○
Bb and B :	○●●○●●●○	and	●○○●○○○●	○●●●○○○●	and	●○○○●●●○

Major Arpeggios :
C, F, F# and G :	○○○●	and	●●●○	
C#, D, Eb, E, Ab, A :	○●○○	and	●○●●	
Bb et B :	○●●○	and	●○○●	

Harmonic minor scales :
C :	○○●○○●○○	and	●●○●●○●●	○○○●●○○	and	●●●○○●●○
C# :	○○●○○●○●	and	●●○●●○●○	○○○●●●○○	and	●●●○○○●●
D :	○○○○○●●○	and	●●●●●○○●			
Eb :	○●○○○●●○	and	●○●●●○○●			
E :	○●○○○○●○	and	●○●●●●○●	○●○○○○●○	and	●○●●●●○●
F :	○○●●○●○○	and	●●○○●○●●	○○●●○○●○	and	●●○○●●○●
F# :	○○●●○●●○	and	●●○○●○○●	○○●●●○○●	and	●●○○○●●○
G and Ab:	○○●○○ ●●○	and	●●○●●○○●	○○○●●●○○	and	●●●○○○●●
A :	○○○○○○●○	and	●●●●●●○●	○○○○○○●●	and	●●●●●●○○
Bb and B :	○●○○●○●○	and	●○●●○●○●	○●●●○●●●	and	●○○○●○○●

Minor Arpeggios :
C, C#, F, F#, G and Ab :	○○●●	and	●●○○	
D, Eb, E and A :	○○○●	and	●●●○	
Bb and B :	○○●○	and	●●○●	

5. Other concepts

1.1. Incorporating the bending tone fluidly (linking with the note before, during or after)

Fluidity is an important concept that will add more coherence when using the bending tone techniques elaborated here. In fact, their goal is to add musical possibilities and widen the sound pallet of the instrument. It is a matter of including them in a way that they become an integral part of the musical language and not only for momentary effects.

This way, we hope, inflexions, playing with tone quality and independence of musical passages will be seen at in a different way.

5.2. Using the pedal

As previously explained, the bending tone lasts until the bar stops vibrating and the sound simply stops. For all steps, the pedal must generally be pressed since the result is directly related to a good vibration in the bar. This way, the way the pedal is used directly influences the way the performer can play the bending tone. For example:

- A pedal lowered for an entire passage requires greater control over the vibration of the bar with the hard mallet (by using more or less pressure) in order to master the separation of the following notes. For example, the sliding note ends its vibration just as the next note is struck, etc.;
- Moderate use of the pedal can stop resonance that can sometimes persist and frees the musician of problems with absolute control of the vibrations;
- The pedal can also be used to abruptly interrupt a bending tone while played.

5.3 Posture and fitness

Generally, none of the techniques in this method require a particular adjustment in posture. In fact, if the basic grip is already mastered (freedom of movement and optimal posture), this new approach should be easy to include, since the weight, in almost all cases, comes from the entire arm and not a muscle or a group of muscles in particular.

The only exception is when playing a descending bending tone from the furthest rope of the second keyboard in order to strike on the first (inverted position). In this case, the muscles linked to flexing the wrist and the fine motor skills of the ring finger and the little finger will require more attention. It should be no surprise that, just like all movements linked to each grip, stretching is the best way to prevent injury. Here are two exercises for this particular movement:

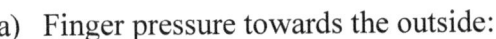

a) Finger pressure towards the outside:

All movement methods help the musician develop muscles that allow him to close his hand (flexor muscles) but do not compensate the reversed action (extensor muscles). The following stretching exercise will help, among other things, to develop certain exterior finger muscles used in the movement illustrated above. To do so, simply use an elastic at the end of your fingers and open your hand several times, as illustrated below.

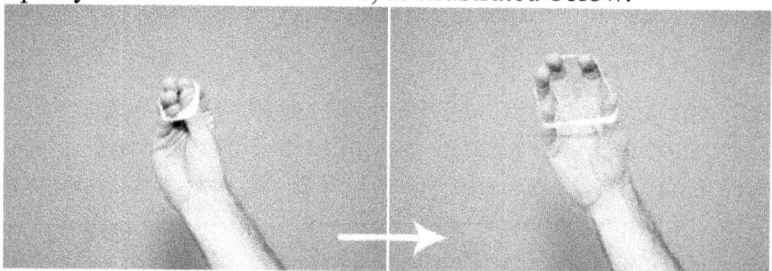

b) Lateral movement of the wrist:

The following stretching exercise develops the muscles linked to the wrists' lateral displacement (abductors (towards the inside) and adductors (towards the outside)) used in this movement. Simply use a bungee cord and repeat the following movement in both directions.

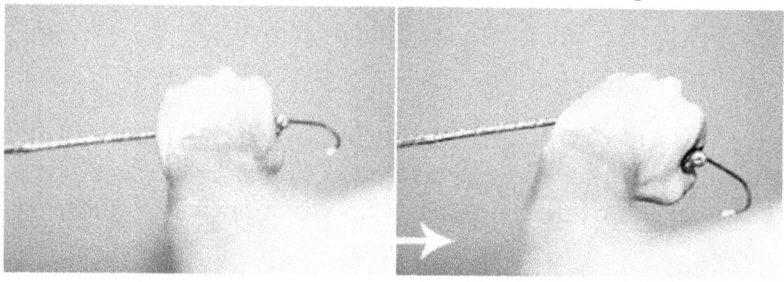

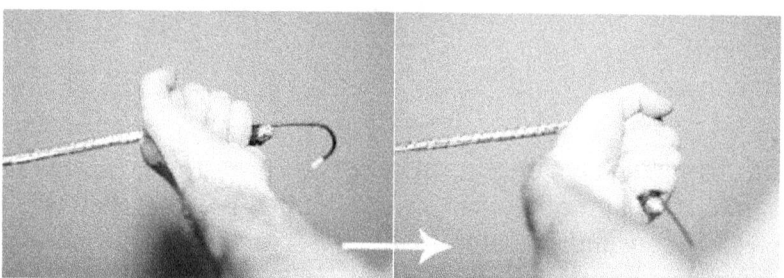

6. Graphology and developing sound

6.1. Graphology
Here are the basic writing tools developed and/or borrowed in order to support the new technical and musical possibilities expressed in this method. All of the illustrated symbols are easily accessible no matter what composition program used[12].

6.1.1. Hand used

○ = Strike with right hand (placement and sliding with left hand)
● = Strike with left hand (placement and sliding with right hand)

These fingerings are usually inserted in the following way. They indicate which hand strikes the surface of the bar and therefore which one places and slides when a bending tone is played. When they are written without any other indication, the choice of the mallet is up to the vibraphonist.

Note: Generally, a musician prefers to choose his own fingerings. Using these symbols is optional.

6.1.2. Mallet numbers
Here is a diagram showing how the four mallets are numbered. They are written above the corresponding mallet[13].
There are some exceptions where two superimposed numbers mean two notes played simultaneously or two possible strikes if the case may be.
Note: Usually, much like the choice of hand, the musician prefers to determine himself which mallets to use.

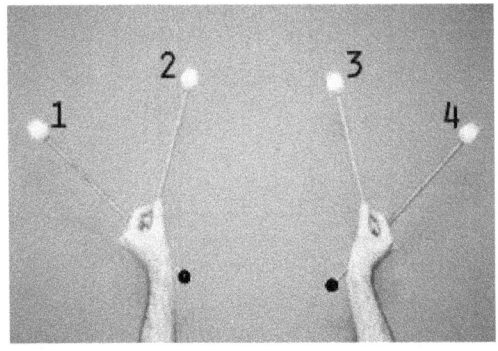

6.1.3. Simple bending tone
The symbol that I've used to illustrate the simple bending tone should meet two criteria: clarity (always distinctive) and consistency (since the bending tone never exceeds a ½ tone down, it's useless to alter its length or shape).

Producing it (length, speed, sound quality, etc.) will be left up to the musician's discretion. It can therefore be attached to any kind of note and will usually be placed to its right towards the bottom.

As for the waiting time (neutreal point) before sliding, insert the sign next to the second tied note like so. In all cases, the musician will place the hard mallet at the first note but will only start sliding at the third beat in the measure. It is important, however, to not delay too long because, as explained before, it's success is entirely related to the quality of the vibration of the bar.

Finally, when writing two simultaneous bending tones, simply tie the symbol to every affected note, like so:

6.1.4. Double bending tone

The double bending tone symbol should be more flexible because it contains three distinct sounds that can be controlled. This symbol has a diagonal line downwards (like the simple bending tone) and another going upwards (for the ½ tone back up). Just like the simple bending tone, barring exceptions, its dynamics will be determined by the performer.

If the three notes were to be rhythmically controlled (original note, ½ lower and return to original note), the two lines must link together a group of three notes (example below), showing that the note is struck only once and that the rhythm is controlled by sliding.

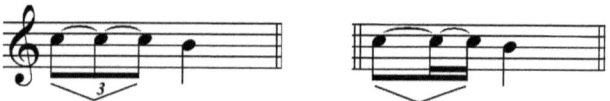

Finally, double bending tones that are controlled but struck only once (back and forth between the two ropes with the mallet) will be written like so.

Note that every arrival to one of the ropes of the bar corresponds to the extremity of one or more of these lines. Varying the rhythm is also possible.

6.1.5. Triple and quadruple bending tones
The triple bending tone symbol is a development of the double by adding another line showing the ½ descent that follows.

The same goes for the quadruple bending tone where another sound (and line) is added. As always, each extremity of the line is a different pitch. Note that there are two possible ways to play them: By sliding continuously towards the end of the bar or by making a short back and forth motion (as needed) of the double bending tone[14].

6.1.6. Off-key bending tones

Symbols of the off-key bending tone are a bit more complex since they require the use of two superimposed values of notes. The bending tone (simple or double) is represented by the longer tone on which different repeated rhythms are played with the mallet, causing the tone to change with the sliding.

Here is an example of a mix of simple alternating and off-key bending tones. Don't forget that the bending tone is always associated to the tone with the largest value.

6.1.7. Bending tone with strike from second hard mallet
The (●) symbol corresponds to the hard mallet that strikes:

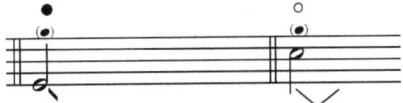

6.1.8. Bending tone striking the neutral point
As for the ▬ symbol, it corresponds to striking near the rope of the bar (neutral point). When these two signs (strike with hard mallet and strike the neutral point) are seen on the same note, the musician has two choices:

   a) **Direct bending tone**

The **direct bending tone** combines the loud placement (normal bending tone us usually silentl) as well as immediate pressure along the rope. It is immediately followed by the sliding motion (a single mallet head completes all of these steps);

   b) **Bending tone with independent strike on the other neutral point**

This one is produced normally but by striking with the other hard mallet on the other rope of the bar.

The first option is the most versatile and it is the one I suggest using when playing them during the exercises pertaining to them.

6..1.9. Bending tones with grace notes
When a grace note also has a symbol associated to the bending tone (simple, double, etc.), it must be played when the note it's attached to is, as illustrated by the example, decomposed before the parentheses. In this case, the strike from the hard mallet must be played with the same hand that slides (see explanation at 6.1.8.).

6.2. Developing sound

Here is a non-exhaustive list of original sound effects to push the earlier research even further. I've also included the corresponding symbols:

a) The double bending tone played quickly and repeatedly (constant back and forth between the two ropes on a longer note) will create a **tremolo** effect like the one obtained from the motor. Note: This effect cannot last more than a few seconds:

b) The bending tone played with the **handle of the mallet on the bar**: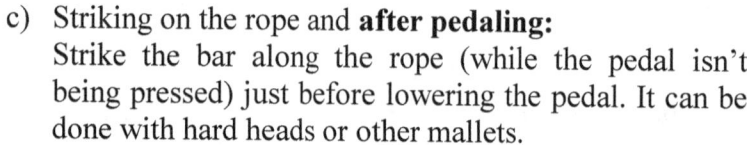

c) Striking on the rope and **after pedaling:**
Strike the bar along the rope (while the pedal isn't being pressed) just before lowering the pedal. It can be done with hard heads or other mallets.

d) **Dead stroke grace notes** with hard mallets.

e) The **delayed strike** with a hard **mallet** on a vibrating note:

f) **Glissando** with a hard **headed mallet**: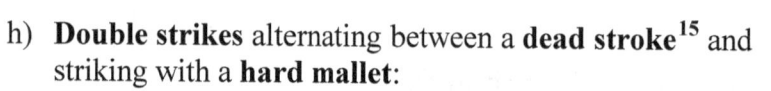

g) **Double-strikes** alternating between a **normal strike** and striking with a **hard mallet**:

h) **Double strikes** alternating between a **dead stroke**[15] and striking with a **hard mallet**:

i) **Accents made on sounds** produced by the bending tone (simple or double):

j) Bending tone with **extra strokes during the sliding motion**:

k) **Harmonics:**

The following symbol represents the harmonic effect produced by adding a little pressure in the middle of the bar with a finger or a mallet (medium hard) and striking one of the neutral points (along one of the ropes).

The stroke played on the lowest note (the other representing what is heard), can also be played with a hard mallet as is the case here.

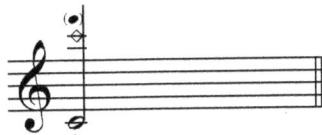

Conclusion

The development of this method coincides with the search for a musical signature (new techniques within the instrumental approach) aiming to increase interest in the vibraphone within the context of musical creation today.

In fact, this new approach shows great potential from an esthetic point of view since it allows the development of the sound pallet of the instrument while also multiplying possibilities for the composer and also increasing the level of technique of the performer wanting to enrich his or her musical vocabulary (flexibility, virtuosity, instrumental possibilities, etc.).

Part two - Exercises

1. Exercise introduction

The second part presents exercises aiming to pinpoint each type of bending tone as well as their contingent possibilities. They are also constructed in a way to naturally integrate the different subjects found in the text. Simply refer to the text for any other questions excluded from the exercise instructions.

2. Exercise guide

The following exercise guide is an excellent way to approach the exercises. Indeed, one should always follow all steps shown by starting slowly and accelerating only if the exercise is mastered, because each step allows the development of the next step in order to control the entire process. Obviously, as time is often limited, you may also follow the steps only partially according to your needs or to the time allotted to learning this technique.

3. Steps for each exercise:

a) Practice the different possible placement **silently**;
b) Practice each movement **without using the pedal** in order to concentrate on the different movements (placement, stroke, slide, leaving the bar);
c) Practice all movements using the pedal and **choking the bending tone in the middle of the bar with the moving hard mallet** (increasing the pressure in the centre). You may use the following rhythmic formula: eighth note (strike) and eighth note (choking the sound). The goal is to practice controlling the pressure and ultimately controlling the vibration of the bar;
d) Perform the exercise but make the bending tone **last as long as possible**. This practices the sliding motion;
e) Include the **delay** into the exercise[16]. To do so, simply wait as long as possible before sliding;
f) **Play normally and accelerate gradually** with the metronome;
g) Redo each step but **transposing** to all possible notes when specified.

4. Notes

- Read chapter 6 (graphology and developing sound) for more information on the symbols used;
- **Important:** Every simple bending tone exercise can also be used to practice double bending tones;
- **Important:** In most cases, there are two possible placements (upper or lower rope). Practice with both placements when possible;
- When the mallet number is not indicated, use the one most convenient for you;
- When the fingerings are not indicated, the exercises must be practiced with both hands;
- Each exercise is separated with double bars and can be played in a loop;
- The beginning of each exercise usually has an example of how to use the pedal. When this isn't the case, each exercise must be played with the pedal pressed and the resonance is only controlled with the mallets.
- The exercises covering all intervals chromatically can also be played in any scale, arpeggio or mode according to your needs;

- Always follow the linear path of the music. For example, if the bending tone is used as a transition between two notes, it should be played so that the first note stretches towards the second.

5. Exercises

Foreword: The annotations which precede certain exercises are either a complement or a reminder, but every step is explained in *steps for each exercise* and *Notes*, introduced in part two.

Musicians aiming to follow a structured process learning to the bending tone should take the time to carefully read them before playing the following exercises.

Simple bending tone

♪ : Firstly, each exercise should be practiced **very slowly** in order to **feel the inflexions leading a ½ tone lower.** Take the time to experiment with the different amounts of pressure in order to be able to play very long bending tones or stifle them with the sliding mallet when desired.

♪ : **Exercises 1 through 12 should be transposed in all keys and keyboard ranges**

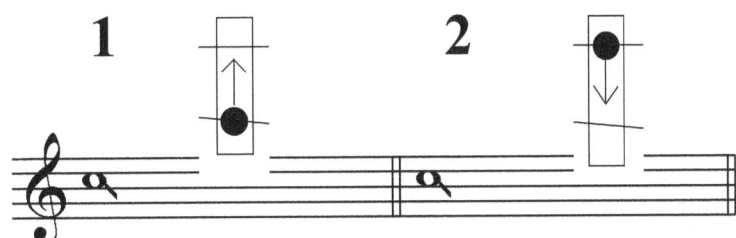

♪: **Pay close attention to the linear path of the music.** The bending tone is a link between two notes and must be "guided" and/or "stretched" towards the next note;

♪: With the **the choking done with the sliding mallet**, the sound of the first note should stop as soon as the second one is struck.

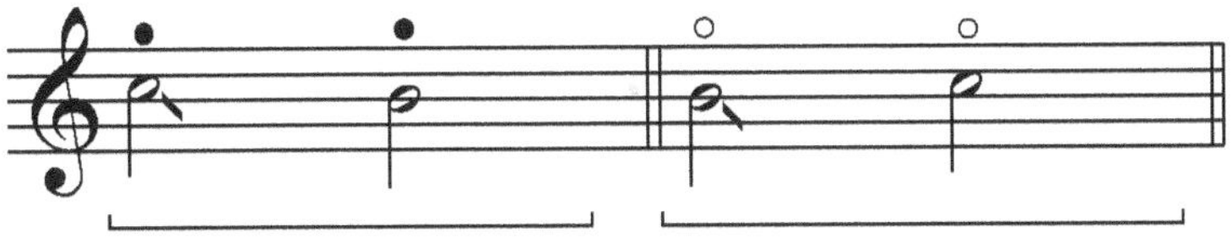

Simple bending tone with rotation of the striking hand

♫: **Similar exercises with a rotation** of the hand striking the bar.

9

10

11

12

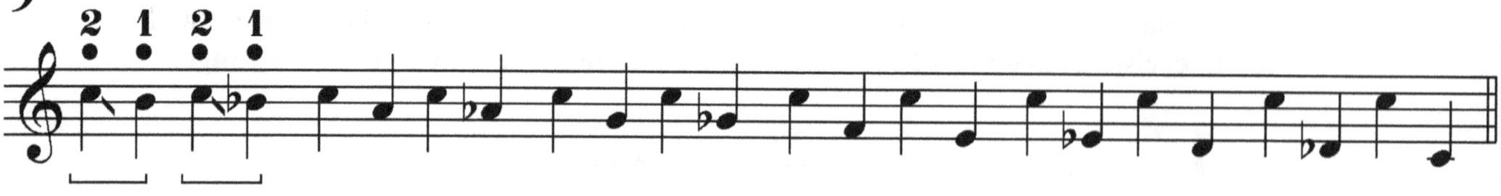

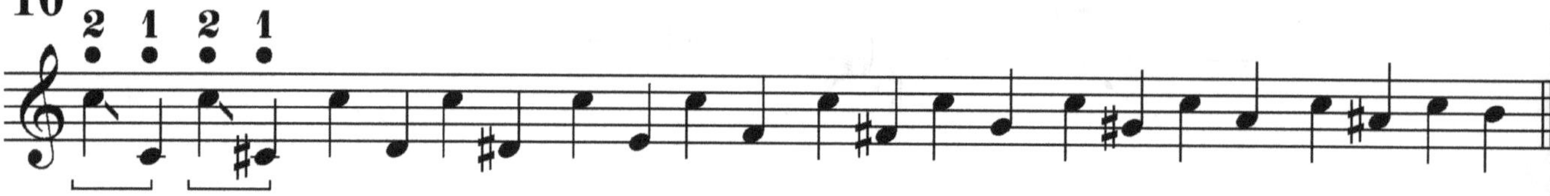

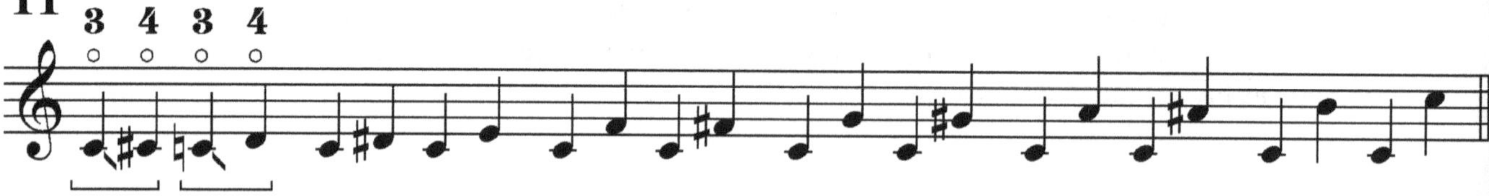

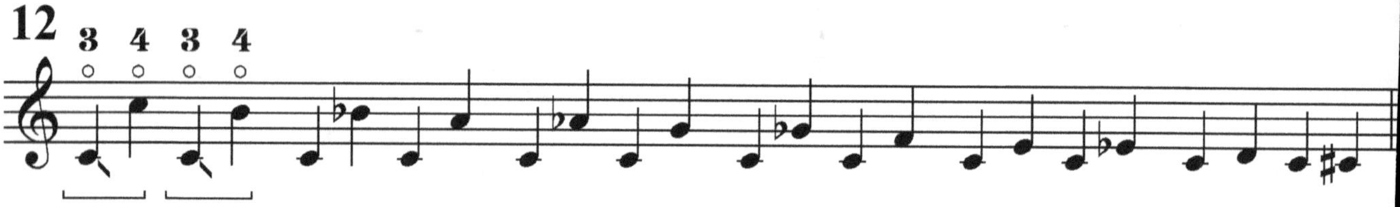

Sliding and striking the next note with the same hand

♫: Pay attention to the evenness of the sound.

1 2 3 4

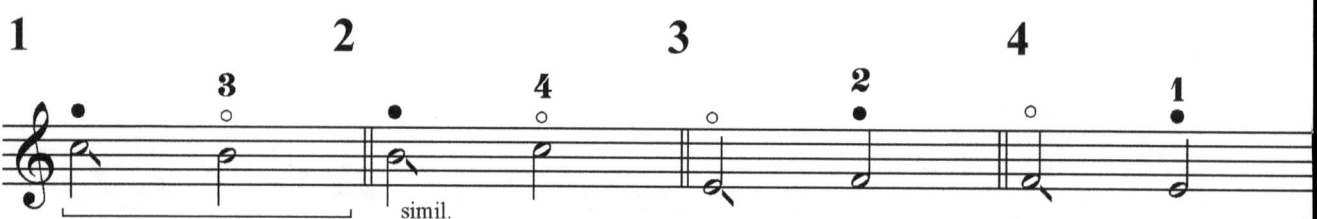

♫ : During the following exercises, **the second note is struck** on the edge of the bar.

5 6 7 8

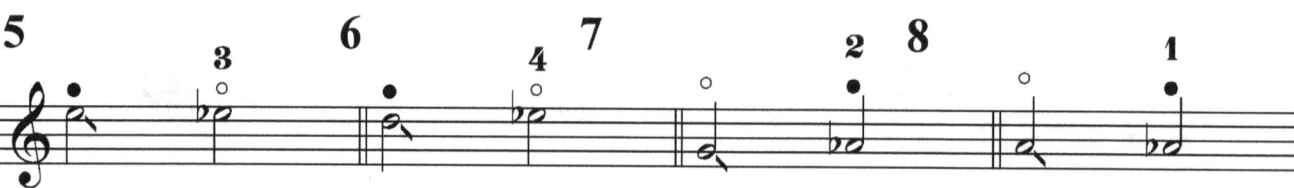

♪ : Exercises to master in **inverted position starting from the furthest rope** (the most efficient) **and in normal position** (requires choking the note).

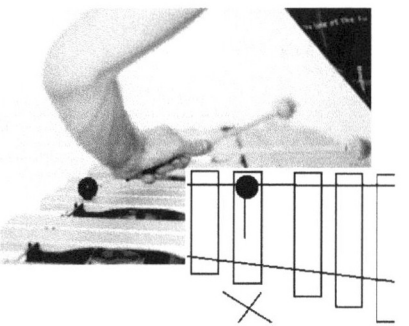

♪ :**Exercises 25 to 72 should be transposed in all keys and keyboard ranges;**
♪ : **Mallet numbers are suggestions only**. Depending on the transposition, the choice of mallets, the placement and the strike should be adjusted;

Sliding and striking the next note with the same hand (sequencing)

♪ : **Exercises 73 to 80 should be transposed in all keys and keyboard ranges;**

♪ : It is important to choose the most strategic placement in order to play the exercise as fluidly as possible;

♪ : **Repeat each exercise** as needed, then play exercises 73 to 80 linked together without stopping.

Alternating bending tones
Basic possibilities:

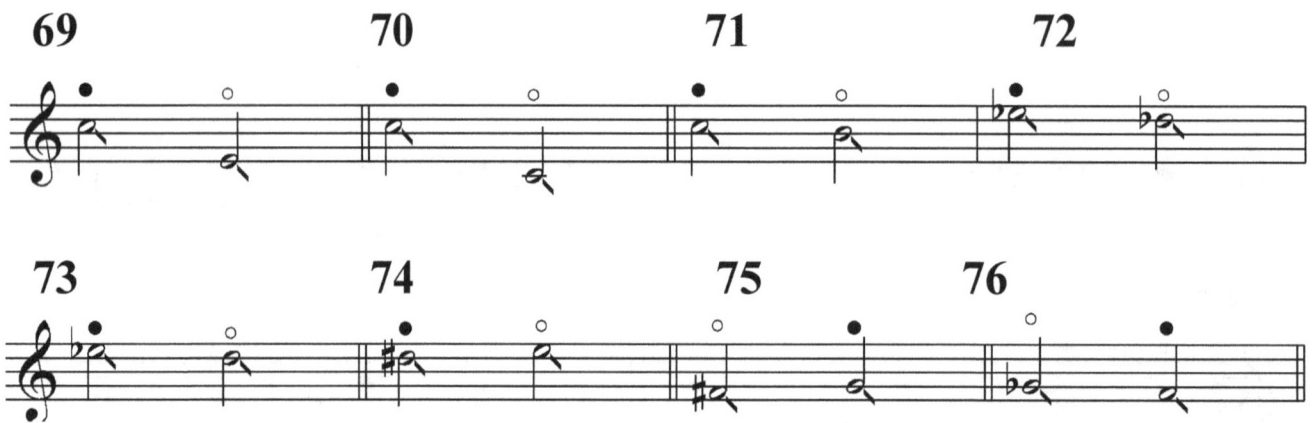

All possibilities:

♪: **Exercises 89 to 114 should be transposed in all keys and keyboard ranges;**
♪: It is important to choose the most strategic placement in order to play the exercise as fluidly as possible.

81 **82** **83** **84**

85 **86** **87** **88**

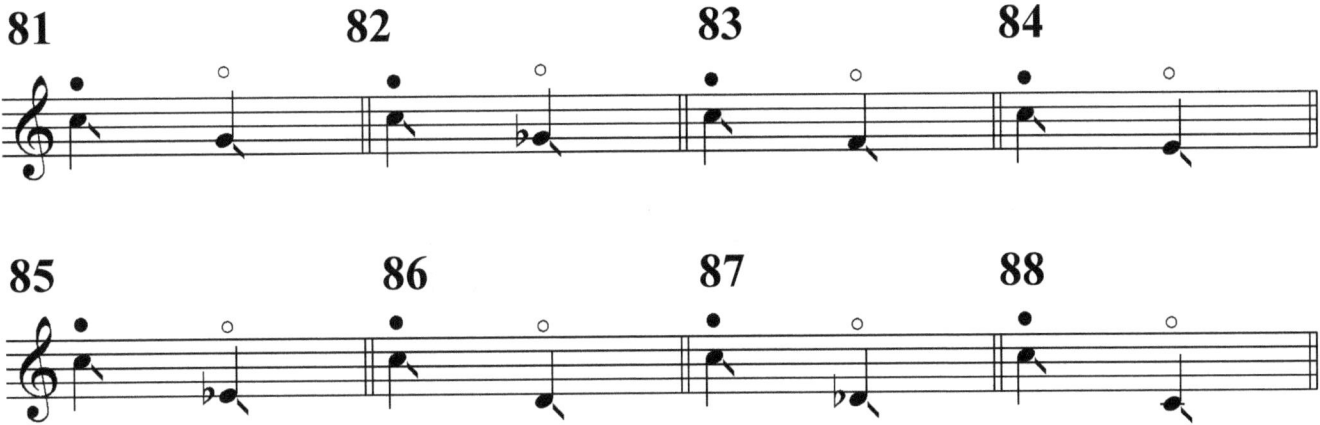

Chromatic exercises (also possible in any scale, mode or arpeggio)

♫: **Rotating** and **inverted position** movements are necessary in some places;

♫: **Repeat each exercise** as needed, then play exercises 101 to 114 linked together without stopping.

89

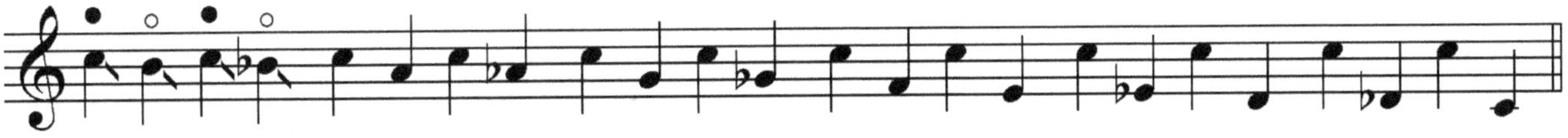

90

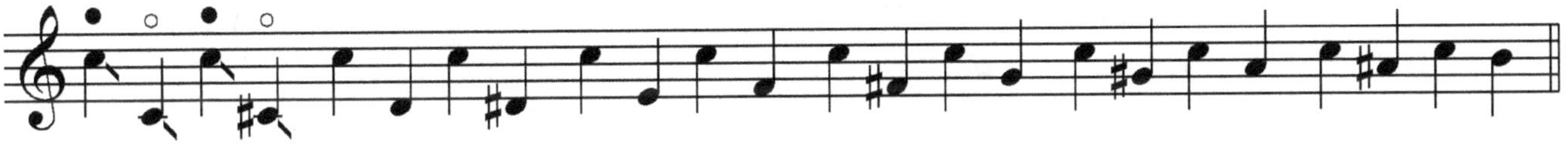

91

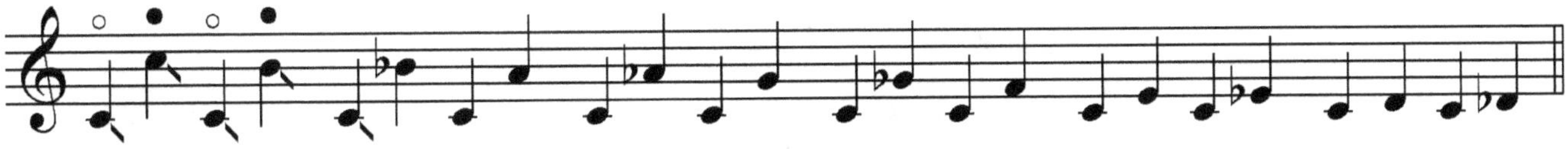

92

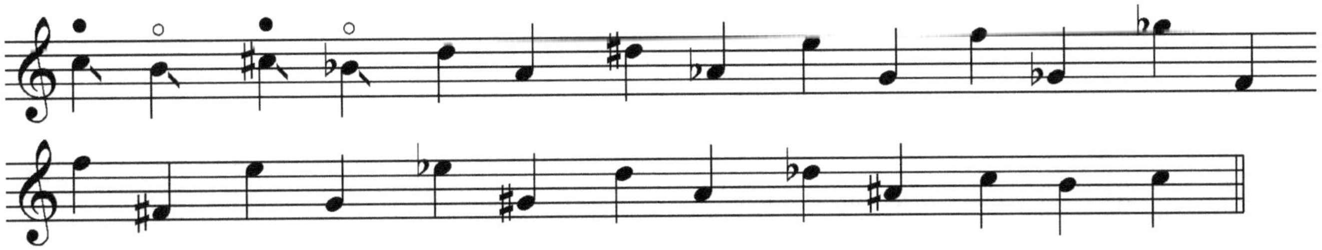

Sliding and striking two notes simultaneously with the same hand

♪ : Use the **inverted position when needed**;
♪ : Some transpositions require a **greater displacement, which chokes the sound** (as short as possible) between the bending tone and the group notes;
♪ : **Pay close attention to the evenness of the sound between the bending tone and the group of notes.**

Slide followed by a four-note chord

Two joint bending tones with slide played with same hand (including keyboard changes)[17]

♪: **Repeated note** with **placement permutations** (see illustration associated with each note);

♪: **Repeat Exercises 153 and 154 until they are fluidly executed** and that the quality of the bending tone is the same no matter the placement;

♪: **Pay close attention to the striking mallet** that must avoid the mallet playing the bending tone in order to strike the same area (the center). Secondly, it is also possible to play these exercises by striking on the extremities of the bar.

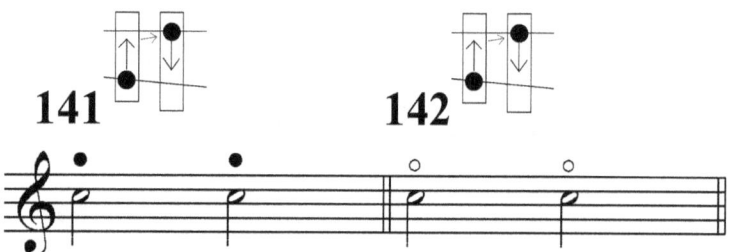

♪: **Permutations: Two successive notes** with **four placement permutations** (see illustrations associated with each of these notes);

♪: Exercises 155-162 must also be mastered **going downwards**.

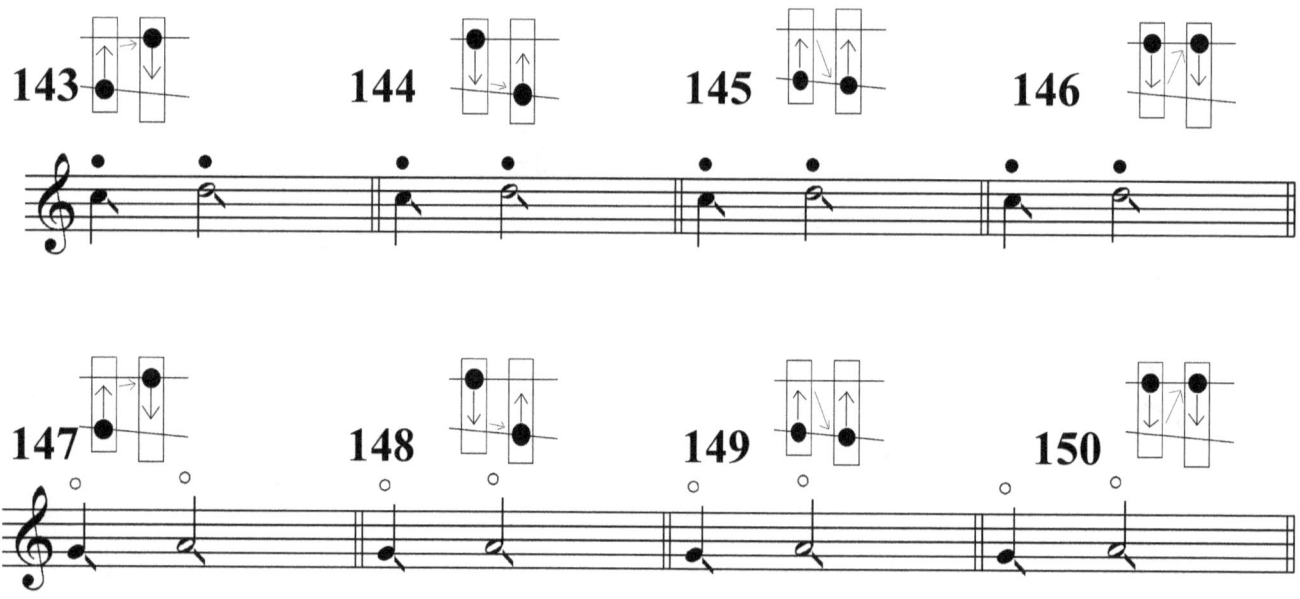

---

[17]

♪: **Two successive notes on two different keyboards** (see illustrations associated with each note or group of notes).

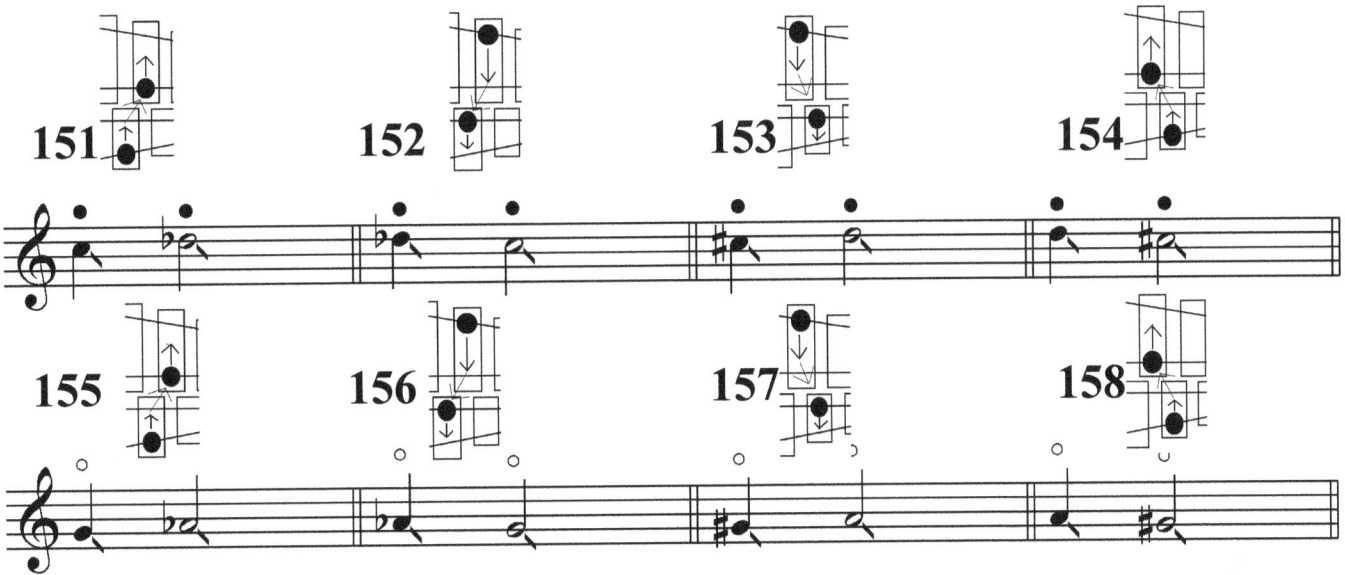

♪: **Two successive notes** (switching hands);

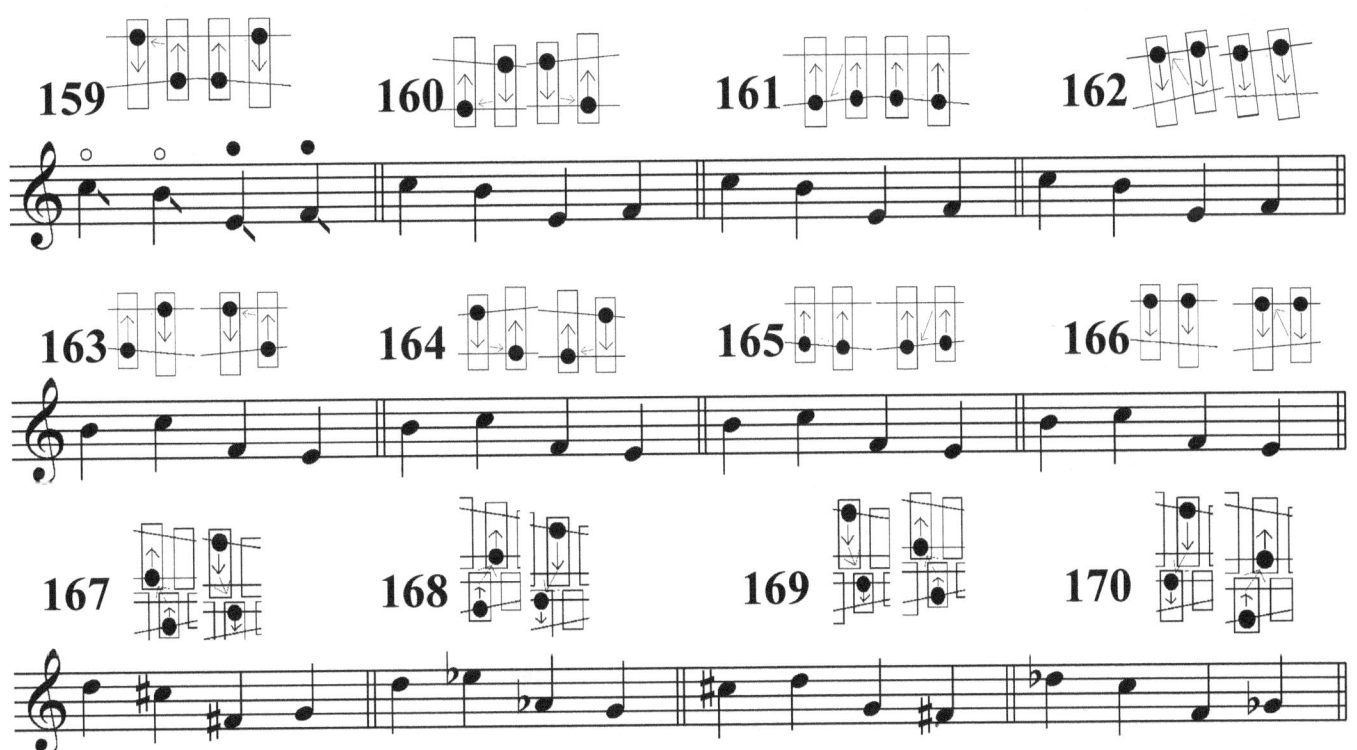

171

172

Three joint bending tones with slide played with same hand (including keyboard changes)

♪: **Permutations:** Three successive notes with six placement permutations (see illustration associated with each group of notes).

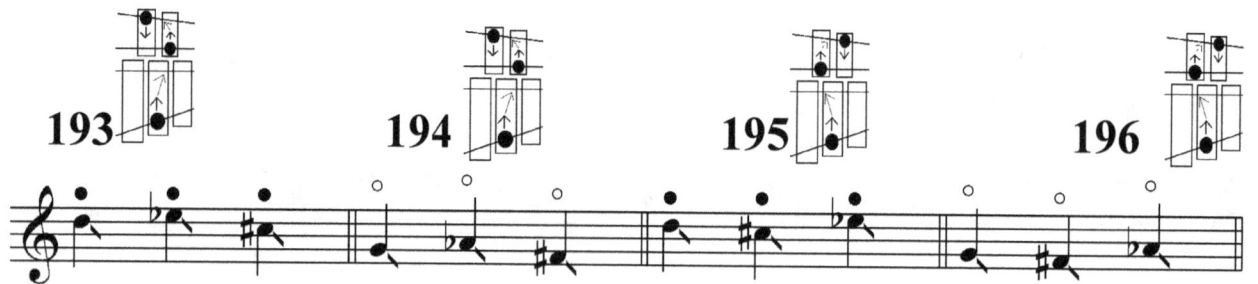

Several joint bending tones with slide played with the same hand.

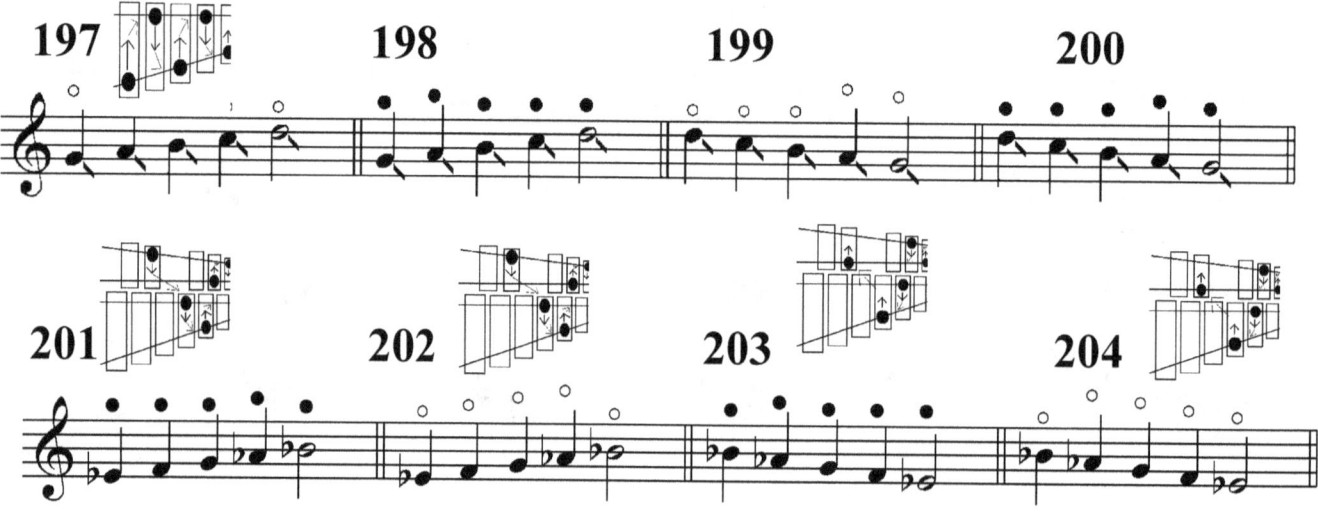

Two separate bending tones with slide played with the same hand (including keyboard changes)

Loop exercise (in 8 shape)

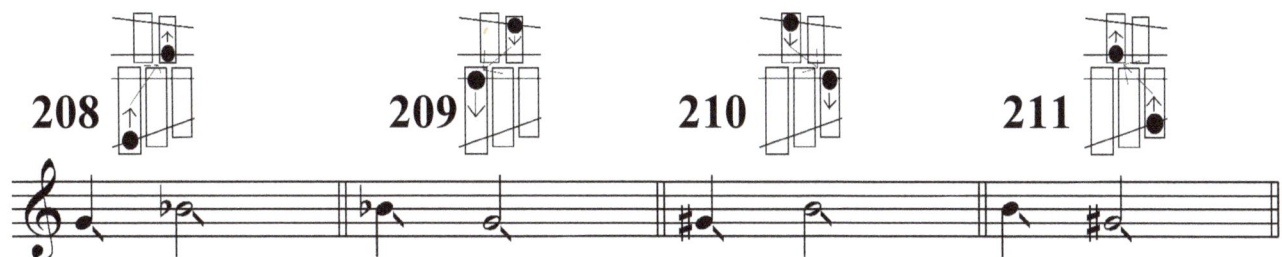

Bending tone melodic lines with pedal

♫: Three examples of possible fingerings in **major keys**;
♫: Emphasize the **contrast between the pedal note in large values** and the bending tone **melodic line**.

♫ : Three examples of possible fingerings in **minor keys**;

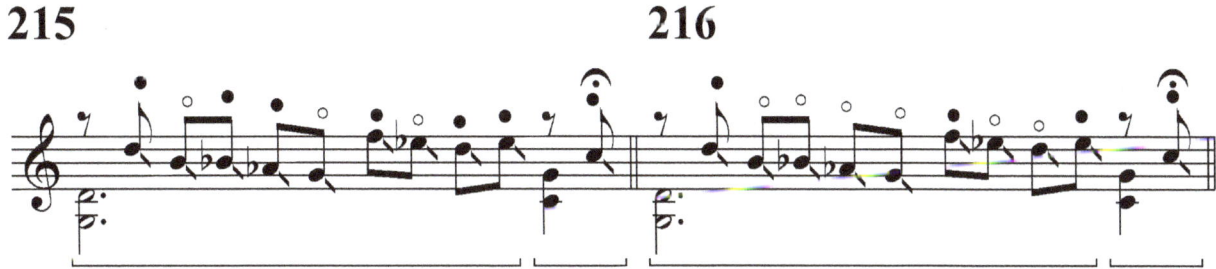

Bending tone with delay

♪ : **Reference**: delaying (neutral) before playing the bending tone (2.3.3.1.);
♪ : Delay as long as possible before sliding. **Pay attention to proper placement**. It is crucial to play this effect properly;
♪ : **This exercise should be transposed in all keys and keyboard ranges.**

Parallel bending tones (simultaneous)

♪ : **Reference:** transition, fingerings, graphology and developing sound (chapters 4 and 6)
♪ : Use the **inverted position when necessary.**

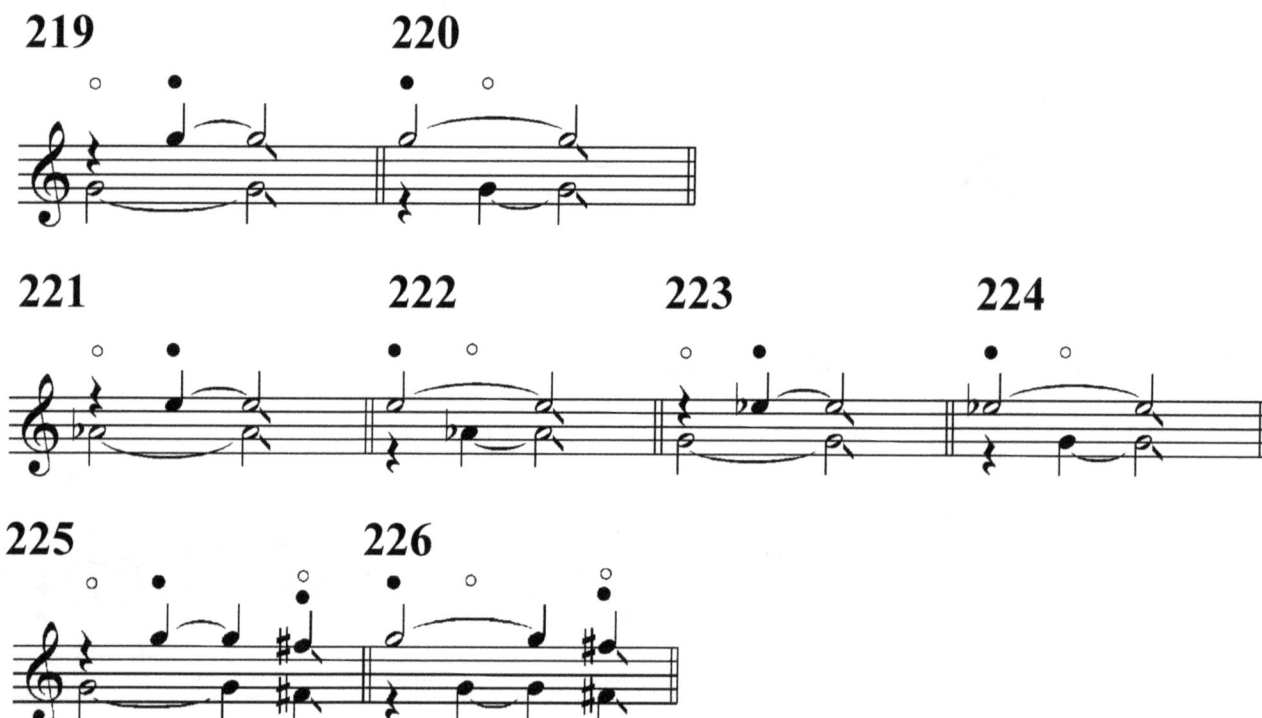

240

Double bending tones

♪ : **Reference:** Transition, fingerings, graphology and developing sound (chapters 4 and 6);
♪ : **Important:** All simple bending tone exercises (no.1 to 252) can be practiced as double bending tones;
♪ : **The following exercises should be transposed in all keys and keyboard ranges.**

241 **242** **243** **244**

♪ : **leave the bar at the rope to let it resonate.**

245 **246** **247**

Double bending tone with tremolo

♪ : **Reference:** Transition, fingerings, graphology and developing sound (chapters 4 and 6);
♪ : Play many double bending tones repeatedly and very fast (back and forth between the two ropes) until the sound stops.

248 **249**

Double bending tone with controlled tremolo

♪: Each new note is played when the mallet reaches one of the ropes (upper or lower);
♪: When the longer note is reached, let the keyboard resonate.

250   **251**

252

253

Double bending tone (controlling the speed according to a written rhythm)

♪ : Each new note is played when the mallet reaches one of the ropes (upper or lower);
♪ : You can also play this exercise with any rhythm you choose. Concentrate on the rhythm played when near the ropes instead of on the bending tone itself.

254

Triple bending tone

♫ : **Reference:** Transition, fingerings, graphology and developing sound (chapters 4 and 6);
♫ : Triple and quadruple bending tones can be played in **two ways**: by **going back and forth with a double bending tone** (shortening as needed) **or** by **prolonging the double bending tone** towards the end of the bar.

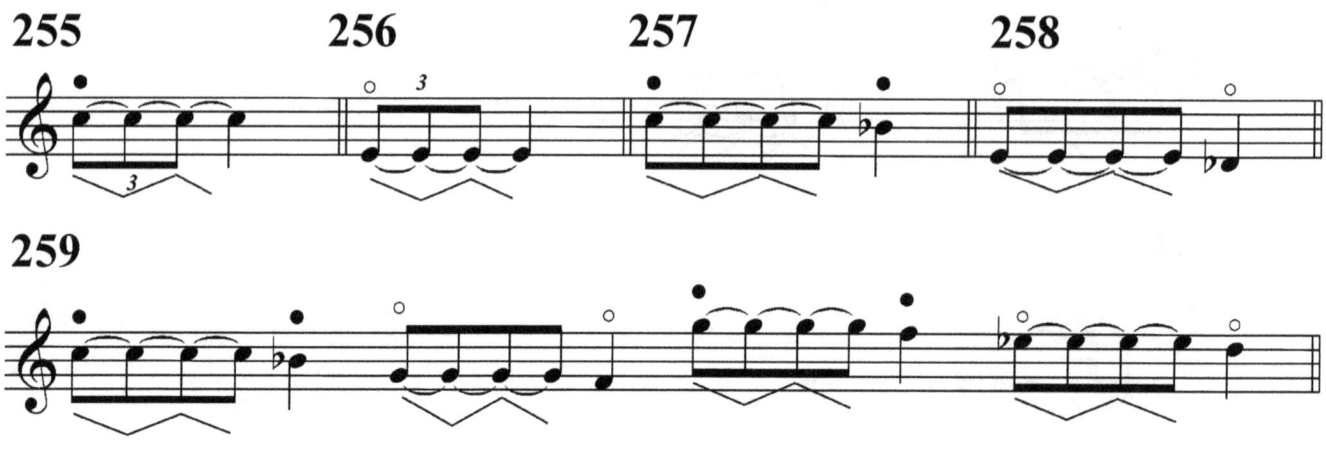

Quadruple bending tone

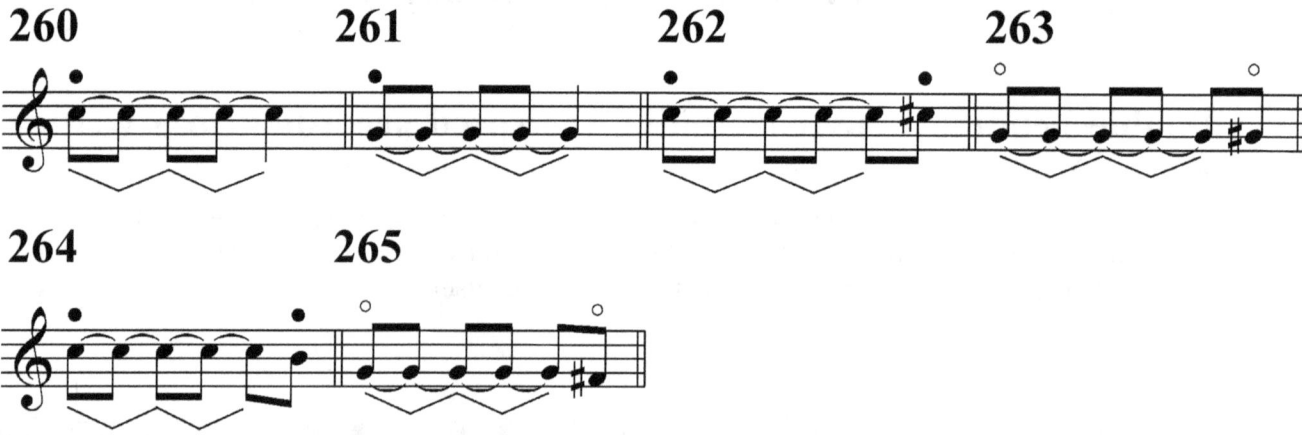

Off-key bending tone

♫: **Reference:** Transition, fingerings, graphology and developing sound (chapters 4 and 6)
♫: The bending tone **affects the note with the longest value** and is played at the same time as the strikes of the other hand;
♫: Make sure to **emphasize the changing sound** each time the note is struck again. These exercises should therefore be practiced very slowly at first.

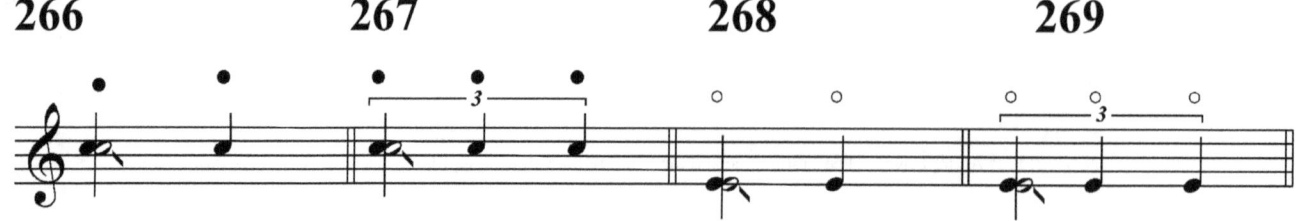

Off-key double bending tone

♪: **Reference:** Transition, fingerings, graphology and developing sound (chapters 4 and 6);
♪: **Similar execution as the previous exercises** (simple off-key bending tones);
♪: The emphasis should be on the rhythm while the bending tone is played freely;

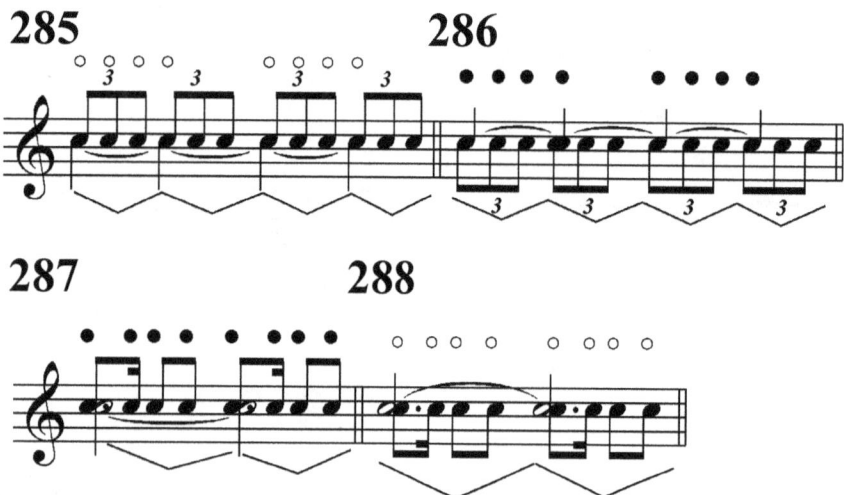

Using the hard mallet directly

♪: **Reference:** Transition, fingerings, graphology and developing sound (chapters 4 and 6);
♪: The (●) symbol means to strike with the hard mallet directly.
♪: The ▬ symbol means the strike must be played along one of the two ropes crossing the bar[18].

Bending tone struck with a second hard mallet

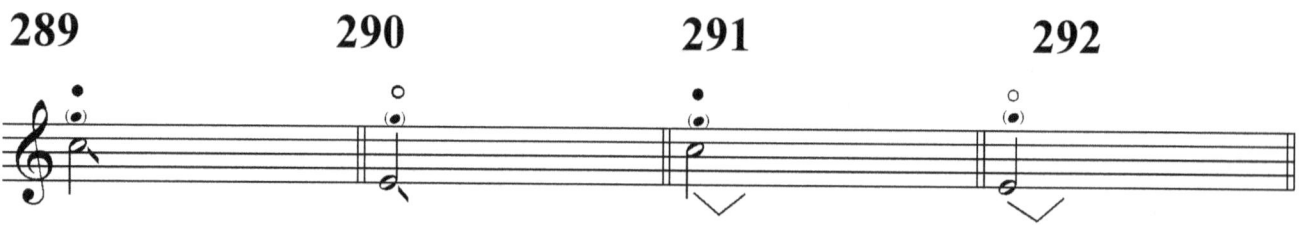

18

Bending tone struck with a hard mallet along a rope (direct bending tone)

♫: **Reference:** Transition, fingerings, graphology and developing sound (chapters 4 and 6);
♫: Even if there are two different ways of playing exercises 305 to 308, they are to be used more specifically to **master the direct bending tone consisting of striking and sliding with the same mallet** (see reference). Learning this opens appoggiatura possibilities.

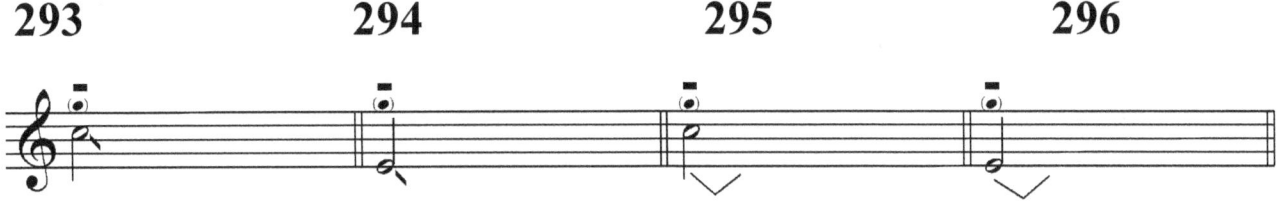

Bending tone with hard mallet striking on a rope (appoggiatura)

♫: **Reference:** Graphology and developing sound (chapter 6);
♫: The following exercises are a **decomposed and easy to practice version of the appoggiatura superimposed on the bending tone.** This way, as illustrated, if the appoggiatura has a symbol associated with the bending tone (simple, double, etc.), it must be played for the duration of the note with which it is associated. Success in this exercise requires the mastery of the direct bending tone.

Bending tone with hard mallet strike on a rope (appoggiatura) - Series

♫: Continuation of the previous exercise.

301

302

303

304

305

306

307

308

Bending tone with hard mallet strike on a rope (appoggiatura between the two hard mallets)

♪: The following exercises are similar to the previous ones but with a strike from the second hard mallet.

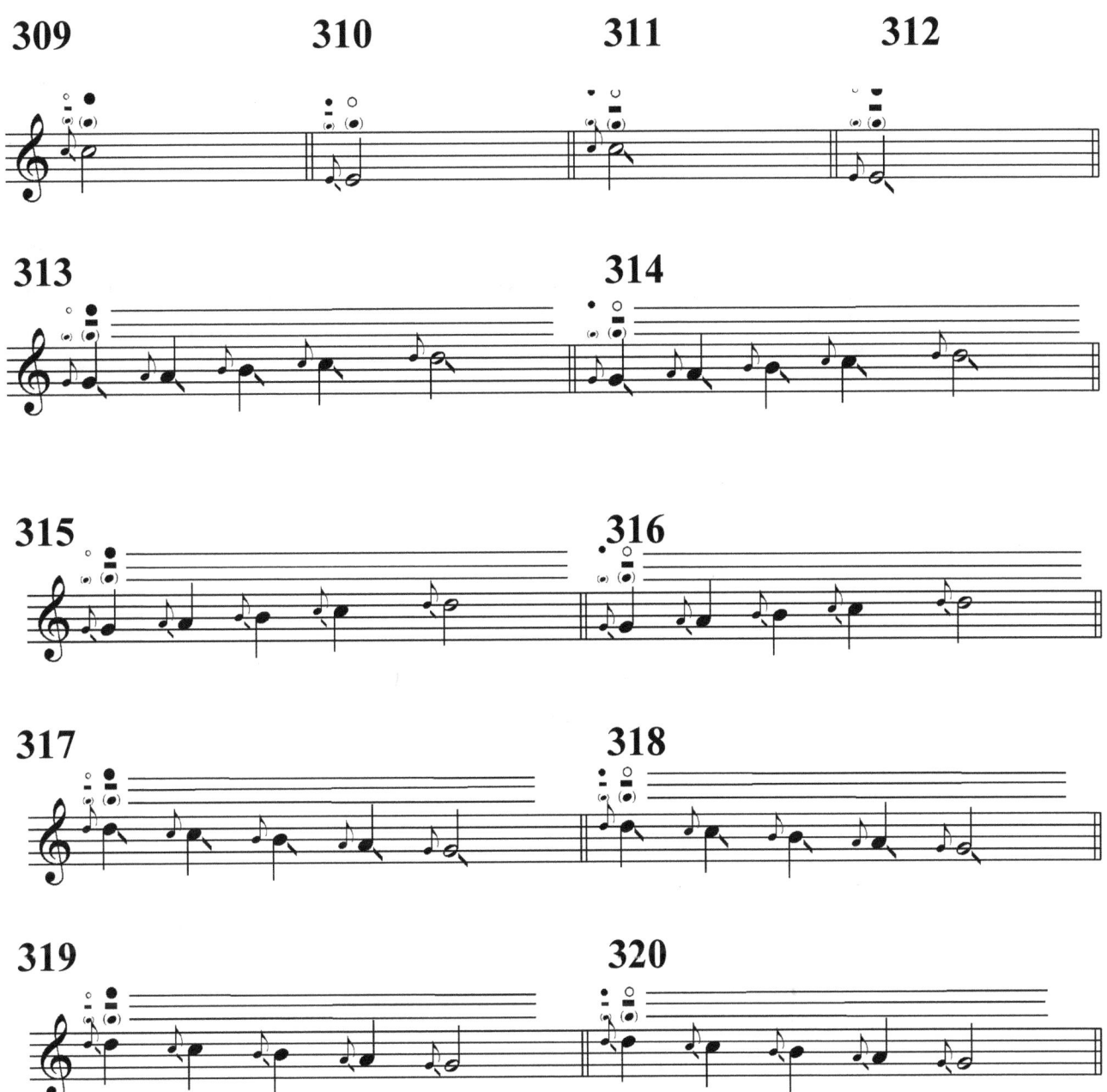

Playing harmonics with a hard mallet strike
321

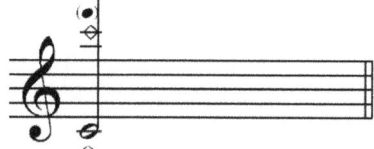

322

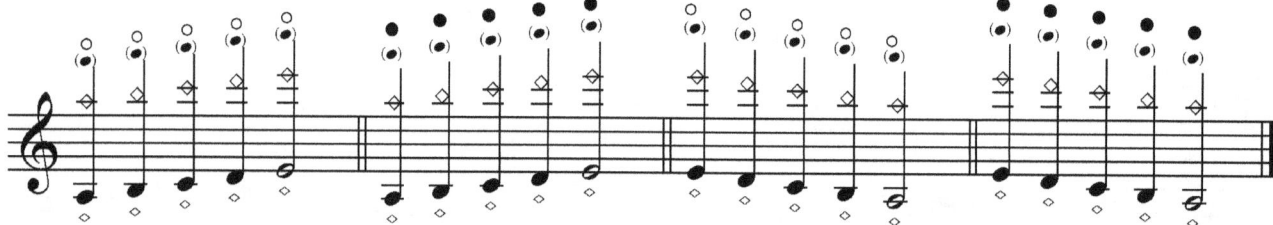

Part three: Etudes

Foreword

This collection of etudes uses the techniques previously studied:

- ETUDE 1:   Alternating simple bending tones;
- ETUDE 2:   Chords preceded by simple bending tones;
- ETUDE 3:   Double bending tones;
- ETUDE 4:   Parallel bending tones;
- ETUDE 5:   Bending tones superimposed on repeated off-key notes;
- ETUDE 6:   Direct use of the hard mallet
- ETUDE 7:   Bending tones with appoggiatura and other elements of sound development;
- ETUDE 8:   Combined use of all different approaches to the bending tone within an improvisation;

All symbols are explained in chapter 6 (graphology and developing sound).
The rhythm of each note is considered free when there is no other information.
The ⸻ symbol refers to a free arpeggio preceding each note. The pitch and quantity of notes is left up to the performer.

The style chosen during improvisation is also left to the performers' discretion.

The X symbol above a note refers to a "dead note" (strike with immediate choke).

The X symbol between two notes or chords refers to choking the sounds while striking the next chord.

ÉTUDE 1
Étues de bending tone pour vibraphone - André Cayer

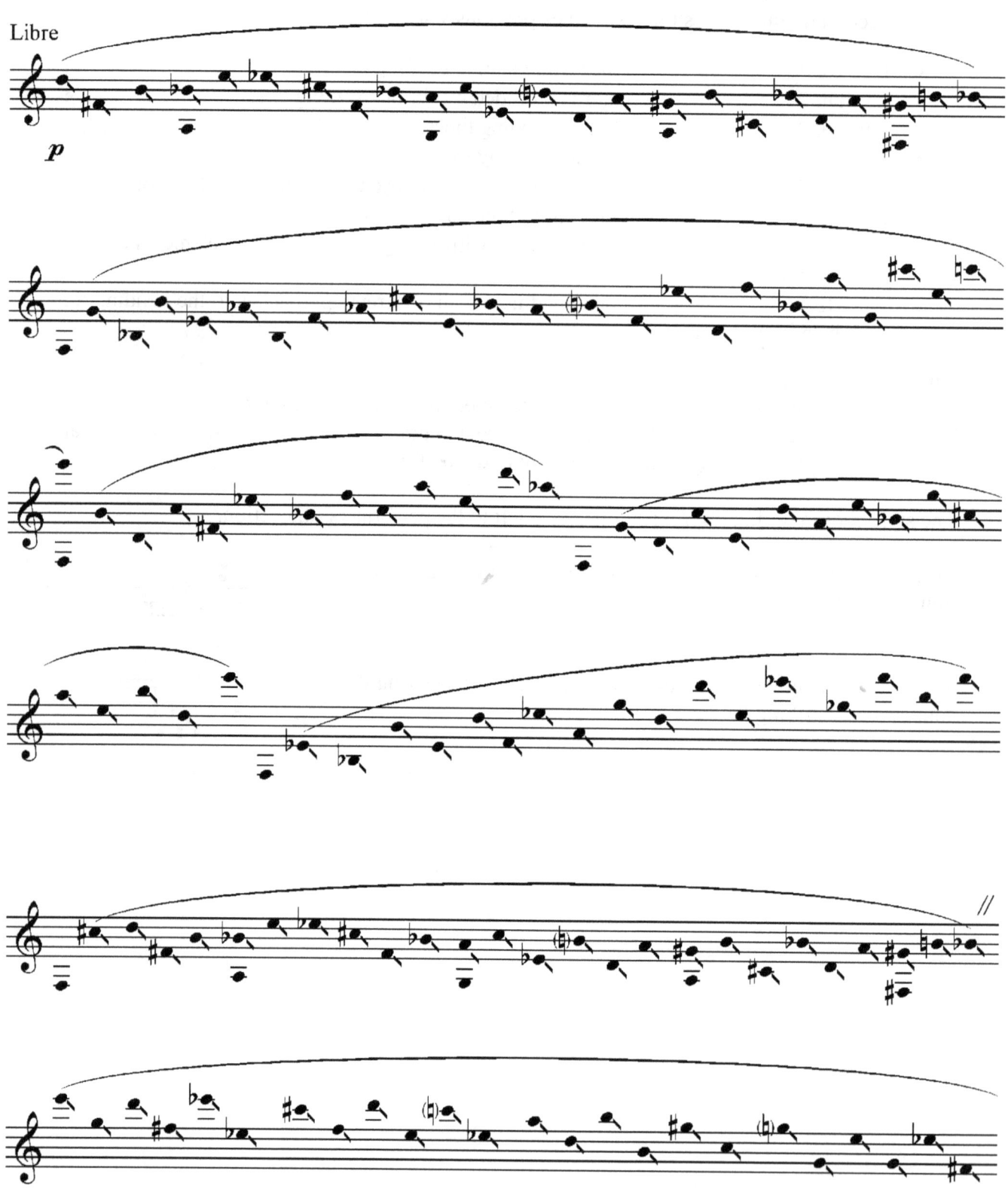

2 ÉTUDE NO.1

rit.

ÉTUDE 2
Étues de bending tone pour vibraphone - André Cayer

Lent

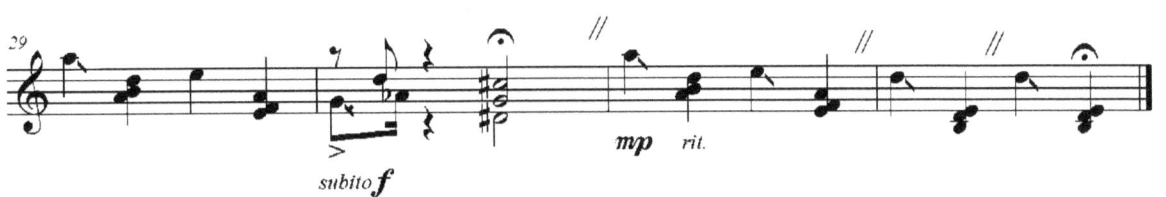

ÉTUDE 3
Étues de bending tone pour vibraphone - André Cayer

2 ETUDE NO.3

ÉTUDE 4

Étues de bending tone pour vibraphone - André Cayer

Lent et libre

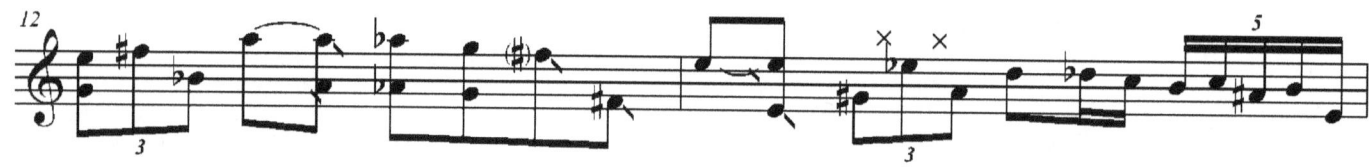

2 ÉTUDE NO.4

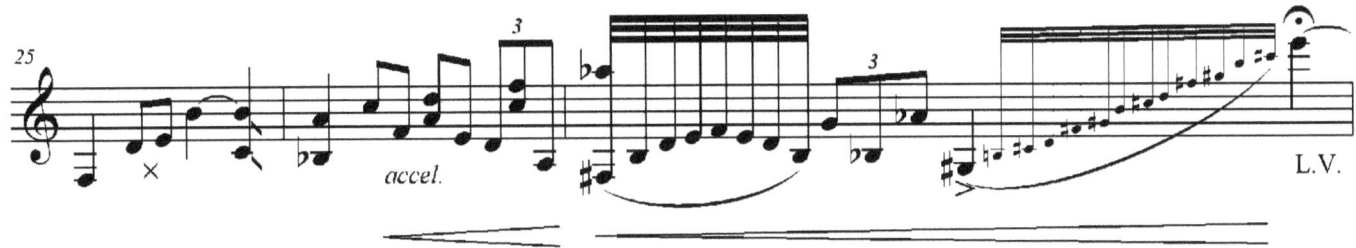

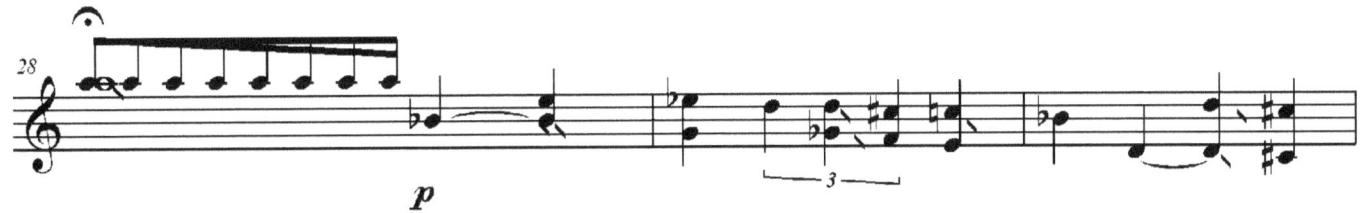

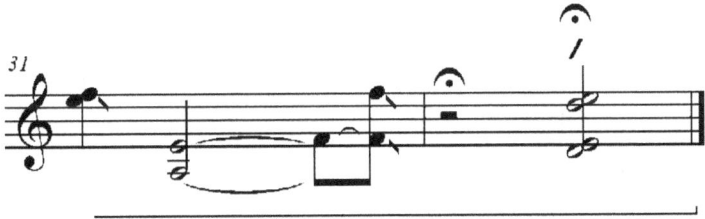

ÉTUDE 5
Étues de bending tone pour vibraphone - André Cayer

2 ÉTUDE NO.5

ÉTUDE 6
Étues de bending tone pour vibraphone - André Cayer

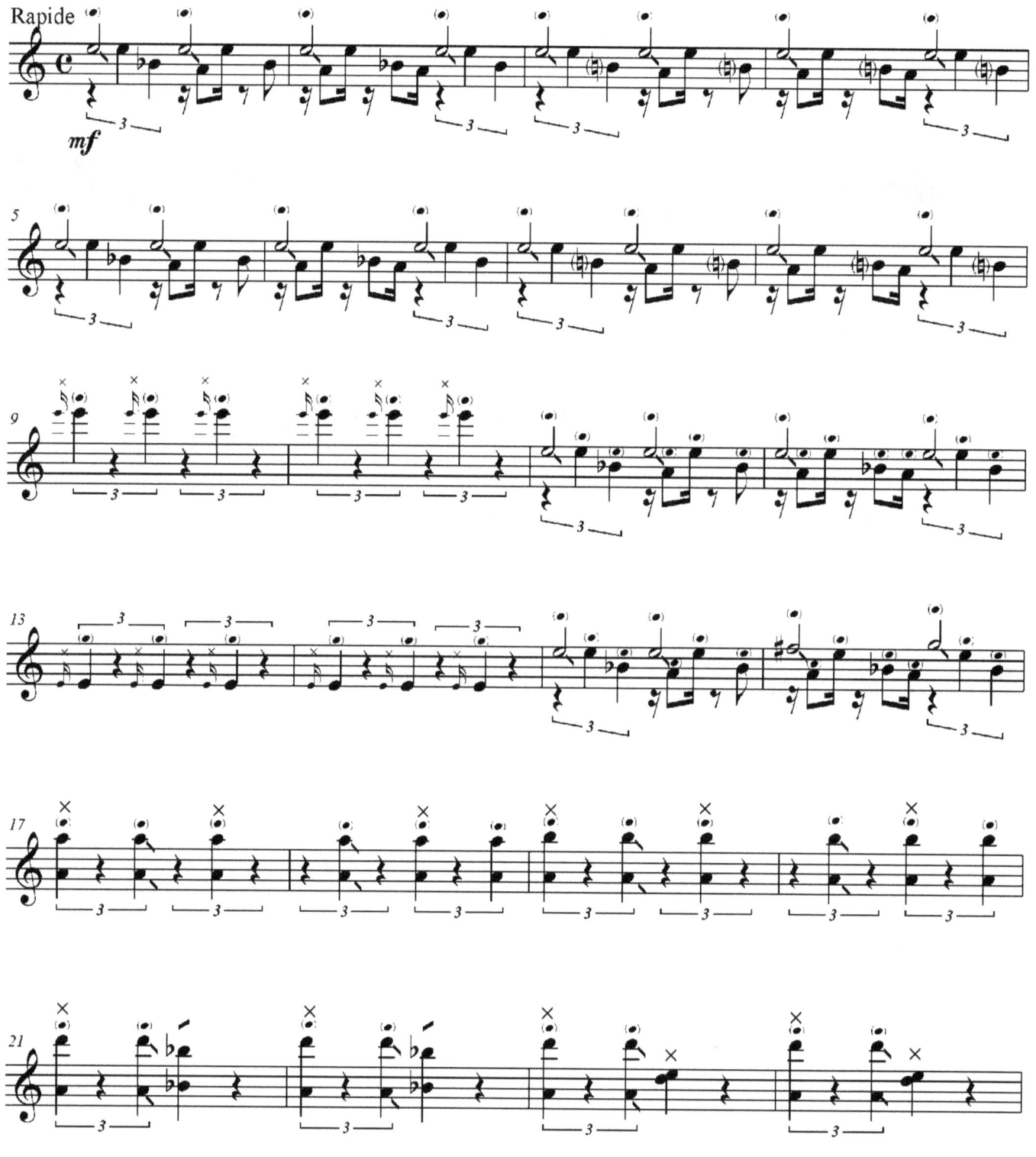

2 ETUDE NO.6

ÉTUDE 7
Étues de bending tone pour vibraphone - André Cayer

www.ingramcontent.com/pod-product-compliance
Lightning Source LLC
Chambersburg PA
CBHW080601090426
42735CB00016B/3311